THE ISLAND OF STAFFA

HOME OF THE WORLD-RENOWNED FINGAL'S CAVE

Alastair de Watteville

Published by Romsey Fine Art

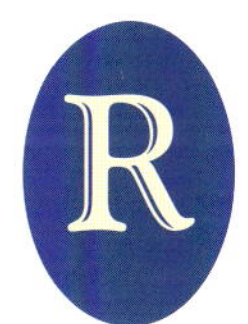

British Library
Cataloguing-in-Publication
Data.
A catalogue record for this
book is available from the
British Library.

ISBN 0 9521517 0 7

Published by:
Romsey Fine Art
PO Box 28, Romsey
Hampshire, SO51 0ZF

Designed by:
David Trotman and
Michael Goddard

Produced by:
Graphics Ad Lib
Romsey, Hampshire.

Photographs:
The Still Moving Picture Co.
Front cover
Pages 8, 12, 13, 14, 15.
The National Trust for
Scotland
Pages 7, 13, 26, 33, 40.
Dennis Bright
Pages 36, 37, 38, 39.
Alastair de Watteville
Pages 14, 20, 40, 42.
Walter Bowie
Page 40.
Turner's 'Staffa, Fingal's Cave'
Page 30
Yale Centre for British Art
Paul Mellon Collection.

The text pages of this book are printed on 135g/m² Consort Royal Osprey Satin and the cover is printed on 240g/m² Consort Royal Osprey Satin which are environmentally responsible papers using at least 50% recycled fibre.

Printed by:
Borcombe Printers plc

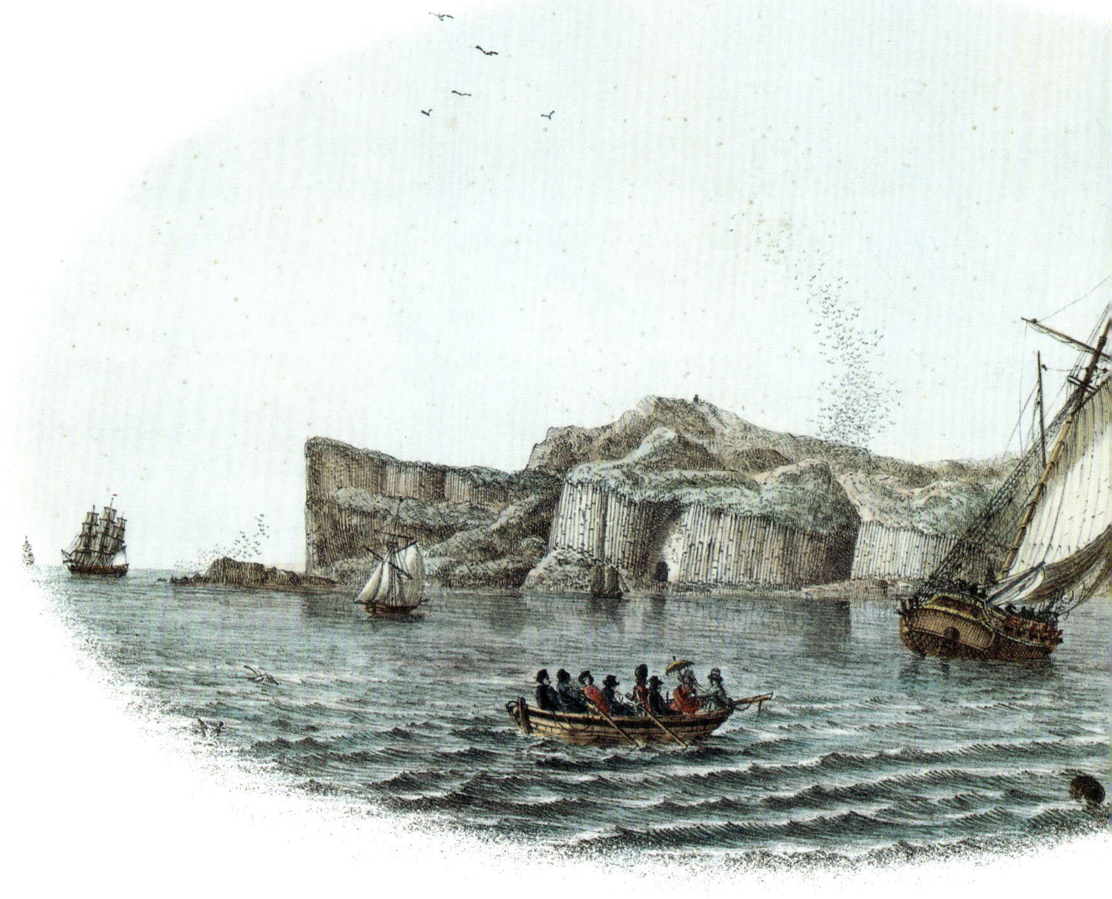

F O R E W O R D

"The wondrous isle" of Staffa came into the care of the National Trust for Scotland in 1986 as a gift from Mr John Elliott of New York in honour of his wife Elly. Since that time, the Trust has followed a policy similar to that of previous owners in preserving the unspoilt natural beauty of the island whilst making access to it both easier and safer. With the help of other organisations and individuals, the Trust in 1991 completed the construction of a new jetty at Clamshell Cave, which, together with repairs to the steps leading from the jetty and improvements to the path to Fingal's Cave, provided safer landing facilities for vistors and local boatmen sailing out of Mull and Iona.

Since the unique features of Staffa were first revealed to a wider public by Sir Joseph Banks, a contemporary and colleague of Captain Cook, in 1772, the island has deservedly attracted a fame and reverence as a place of pilgrimage out of all proportion to its small dimensions.

The National Trust for Scotland is, amongst other things, the guardian of several examples of Scotland's magnificent heritage of scenic beauty. Staffa is one such national treasure and a truly remarkable natural wonder of the world.

Douglas Dow CB
Director, National Trust for Scotland
Edinburgh, April 1993

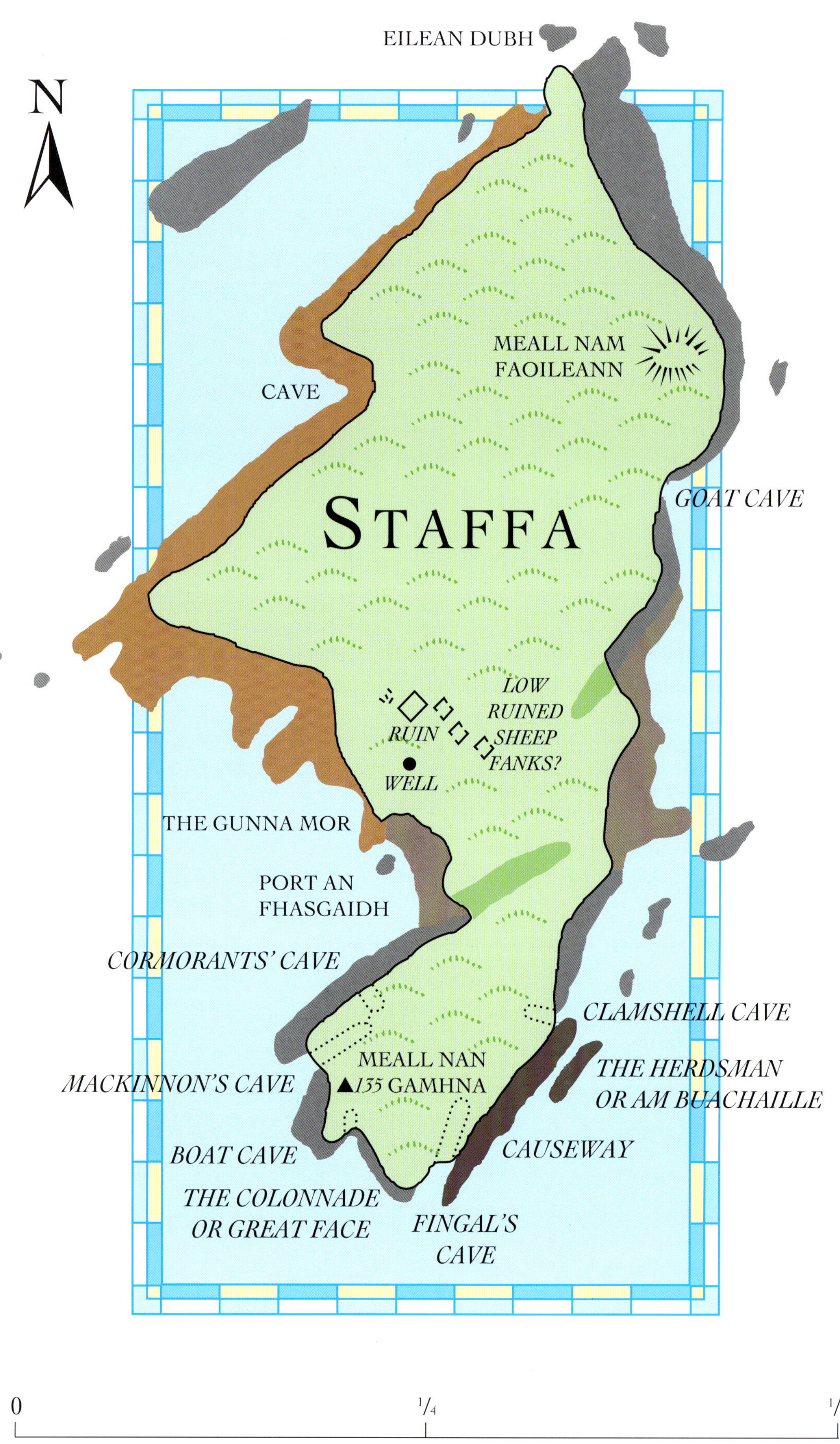
EILEAN DUBH
N
MEALL NAM
FAOILEANN
CAVE
GOAT CAVE
STAFFA
LOW
RUINED
SHEEP
FANKS?
RUIN
WELL
THE GUNNA MOR
PORT AN
FHASGAIDH
CORMORANTS' CAVE
CLAMSHELL CAVE
MEALL NAN
GAMHNA
▲135
THE HERDSMAN
OR AM BUACHAILLE
MACKINNON'S CAVE
CAUSEWAY
BOAT CAVE
THE COLONNADE
OR GREAT FACE
FINGAL'S
CAVE
0
1/4
1/2
Mile

STAFFA THE ISLAND

Staffa is an uninhabited island of 80 acres lying to the west of The Isle of Mull, and about six miles north of Iona. In the rather severe words of The Nature Conservancy it is a "spectacular example of columnar jointing in Tertiary plateau lava flow". In 1973 it was declared a Site of Special Scientific Interest.

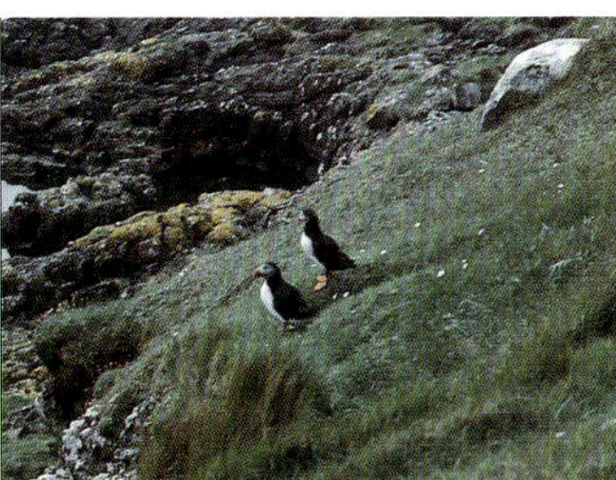

About 60 million years ago intense volcanic activity in the area and, specifically, on Mull, led to a blanket of lava being fed far out into the Atlantic. Most has been eroded and dispersed, but Staffa, the Treshnish Islands, and other small islands have remained as stubborn outcrops. This is, of course, a gross simplification of a complex geological story which is still unfolding.

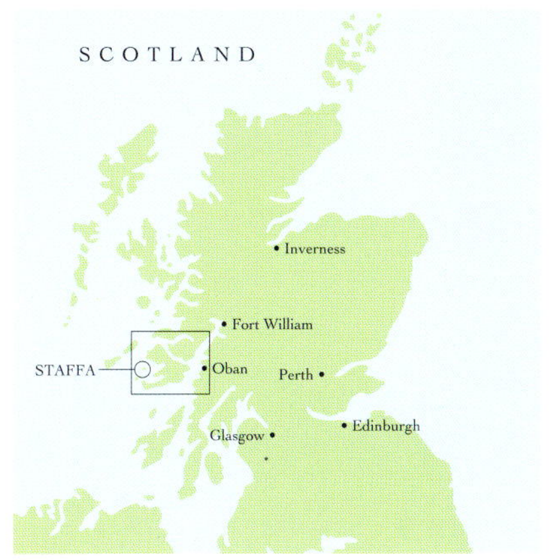

Staffa consists of three layers of rock of different types, covered with a surface of rich soil and lush grass. The lowest layer is *tuff*, compressed volcanic ash and dust; the middle layer is composed of the basaltic columns; and the uppermost is made up of jumbled and fractured columns, and volcanic debris. The whole structure is best appreciated from the sea a little way off the south of the island. The slant of some four degrees downwards from west to east, caused by disturbance deep down after the columns had been created, is apparent. The lifting of the tuff above sea-level on the western portion provided the opportunity for the sea to exploit areas of weakness and so create the three main caves there.

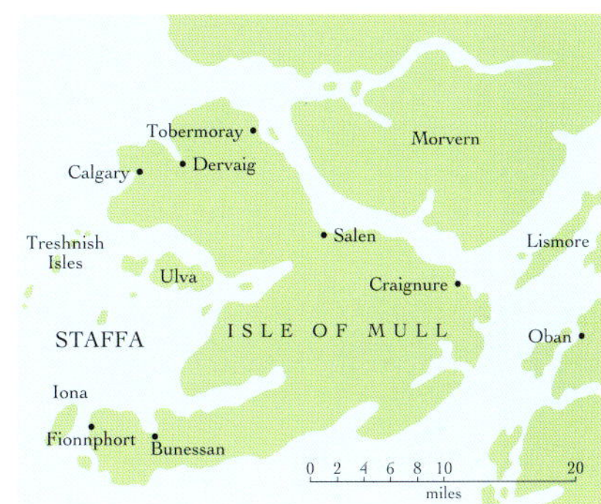

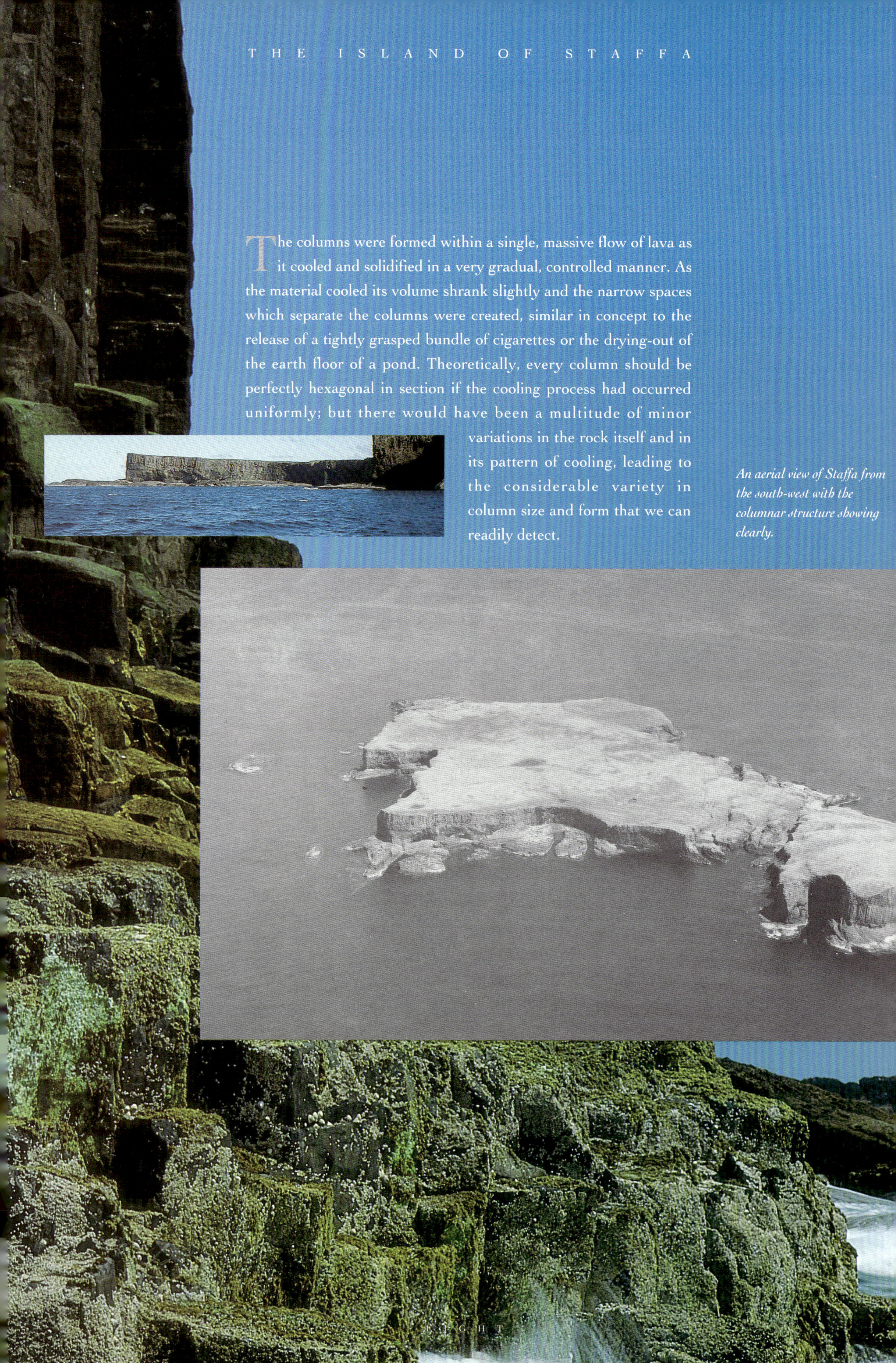

The columns were formed within a single, massive flow of lava as it cooled and solidified in a very gradual, controlled manner. As the material cooled its volume shrank slightly and the narrow spaces which separate the columns were created, similar in concept to the release of a tightly grasped bundle of cigarettes or the drying-out of the earth floor of a pond. Theoretically, every column should be perfectly hexagonal in section if the cooling process had occurred uniformly; but there would have been a multitude of minor variations in the rock itself and in its pattern of cooling, leading to the considerable variety in column size and form that we can readily detect.

An aerial view of Staffa from the south-west with the columnar structure showing clearly.

Clamshell Cave, and the stairway before it was taken down in 1937.

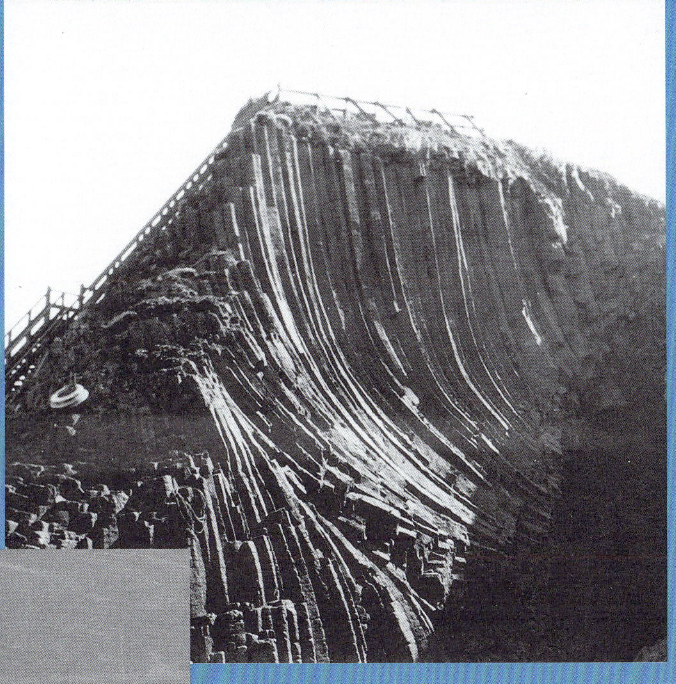

When the columns were taking shape a persistant white deposit settled in the spaces left by the contraction of the rock. This substance disappears within a few years if it is exposed to the weather.

In 1947, when a floating sea-mine struck the southern face of the island and exploded dislodging 14 columns, the site of the damage was revealed by the white scar of the deposit and was conspicuously in evidence until about 1960.

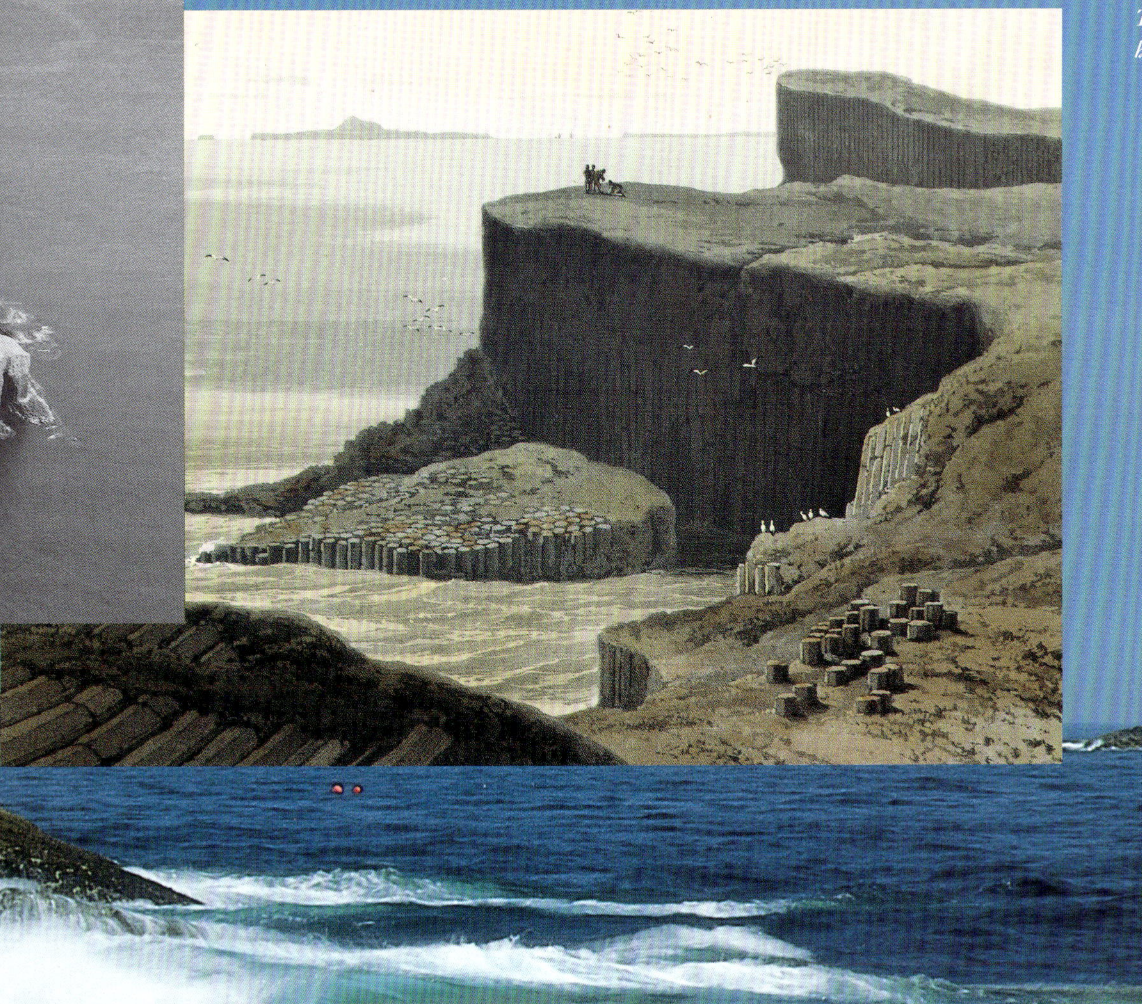

The Old Harbour and western headlands, by William Daniell

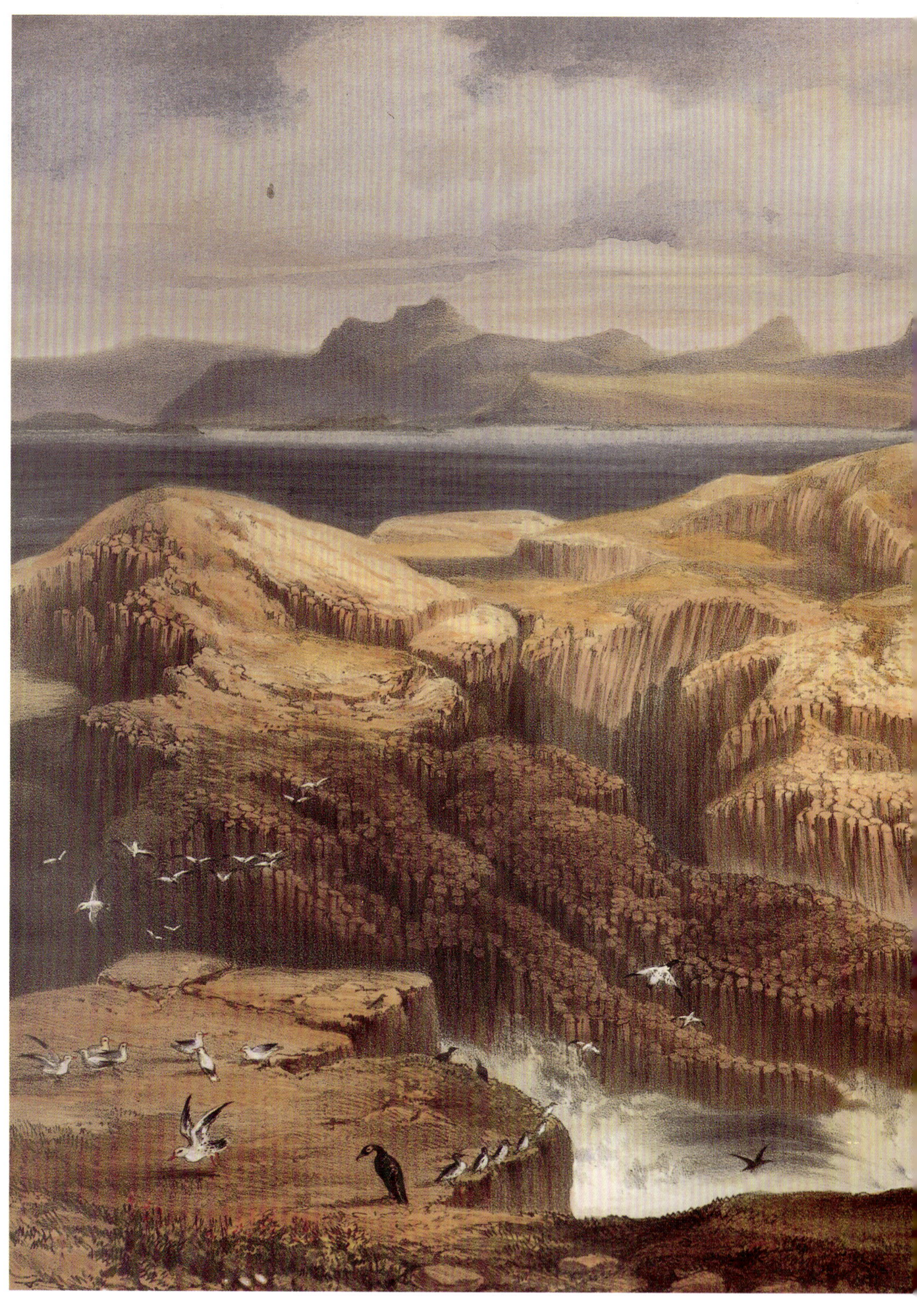

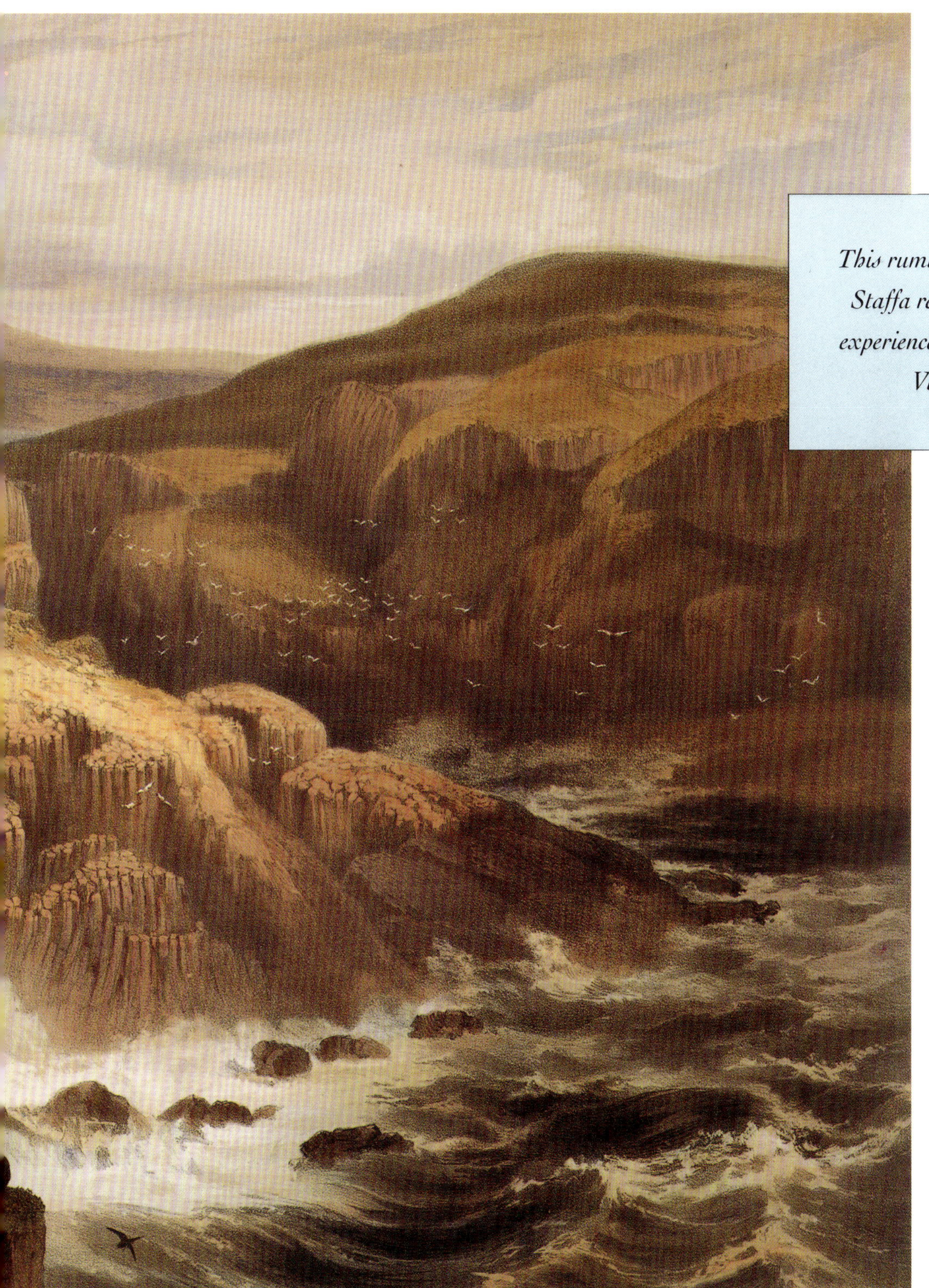

This rumbustious impression of Staffa reflects the excitement experienced by many visitors in Victorian times.

The map on page six shows Staffa's main physical features. The five principal caves are marked, and the Causeway of snapped columns which links Fingal's Cave with Clamshell Cave. *Port an Fhasgaidh,* gaelic for Shelter Haven, but commonly known as the Old Harbour, is the only beach on the island where boats can be dragged up clear of the surf: it is also the destination of driftwood, valuable for anyone residing on Staffa. The highest point is *Meall nan Gamhna,* The Hill of the Stirks (or Heifers), 135 feet above low-water. Two islets are given names on Ordnance Survey maps. They are *Am Buachaille,* The Herdsman, alongside the Causeway, composed entirely of twisted columns; and *Eilean Dubh,* The Black Isle, which is home to several sea-bird colonies.

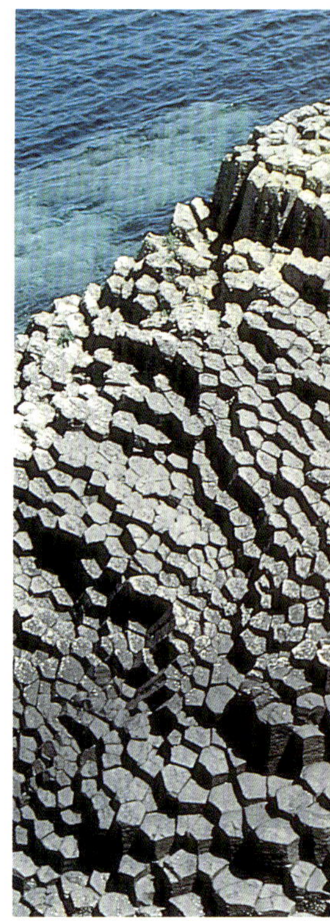

This small islet, formed wholly of basaltic columns is known as The Herdsman.

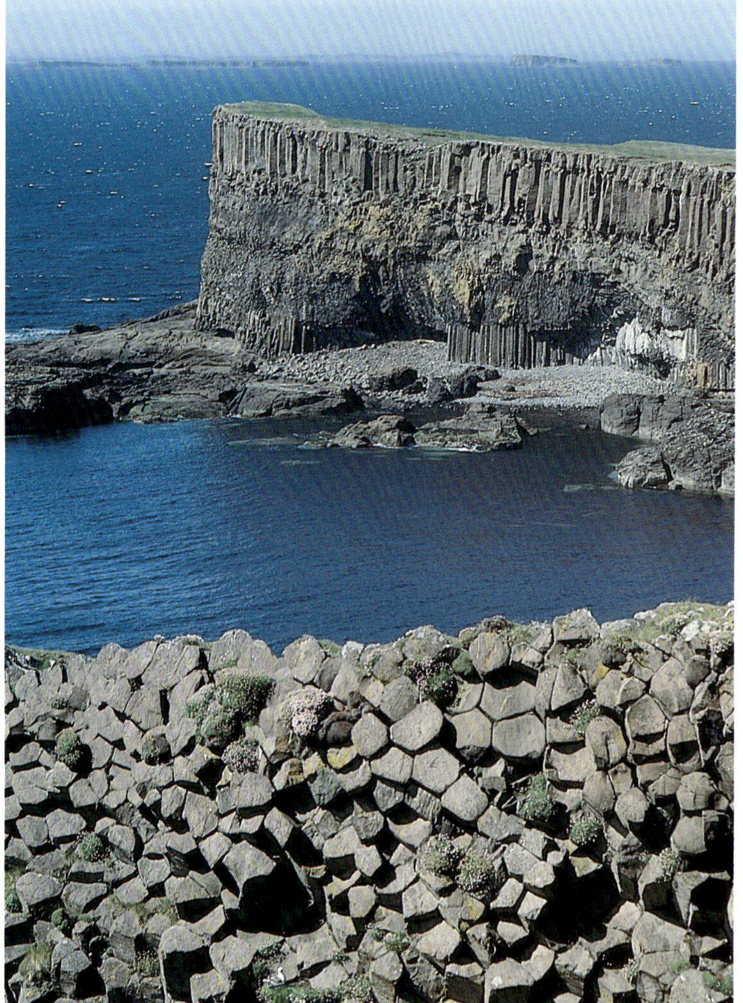

Left: Fractured columns at the mouth of the Old Harbour.

Right: A shallow opening in the wall of columns beside the Causeway known as Fingal's Chair. Wishes made whilst sitting in the chair are said to be granted.

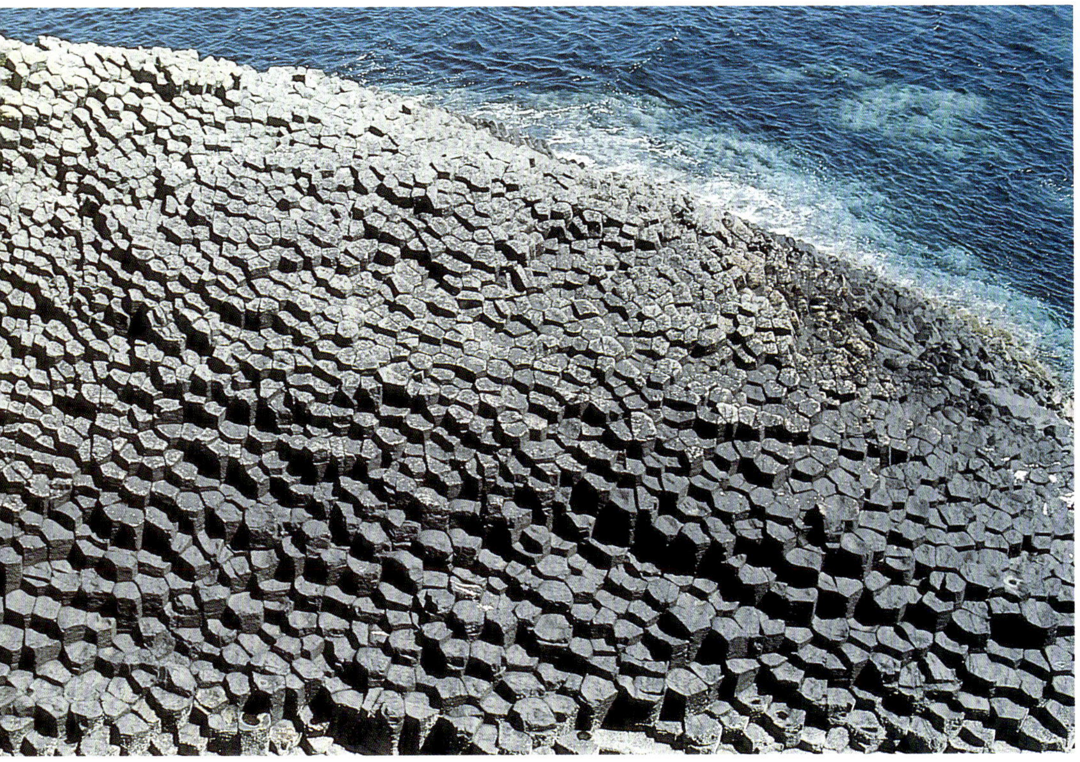

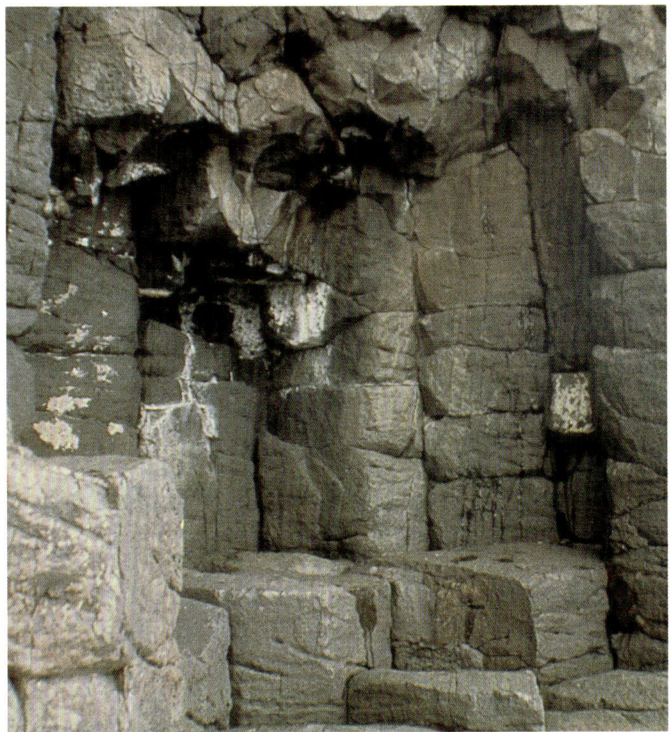

The name Staffa itself dates from Viking occupancy of the west Scottish coast from the 10th to 13th centuries, and comes from the Norse word for the vertical staves used for house building at that time in Scandinavia.

Each of the ten further sections of the book addresses a particular aspect of this unique and beguiling island.

FINGAL'S CAVE

Three strands combine to make Fingal's Cave on Staffa perhaps the best known of all caves.

Its structure is unique. Nowhere else is there a sea-cave formed completely in hexagonally-jointed basalt. To this distinctiveness, drama and intense interest are imparted by the size, the sounds, the colours, and the remarkable symmetry of this 227-foot cavern; and by Nature's gift of fractured columns forming a crude walkway just above high-water level, allowing exploring visitors to go far inside.

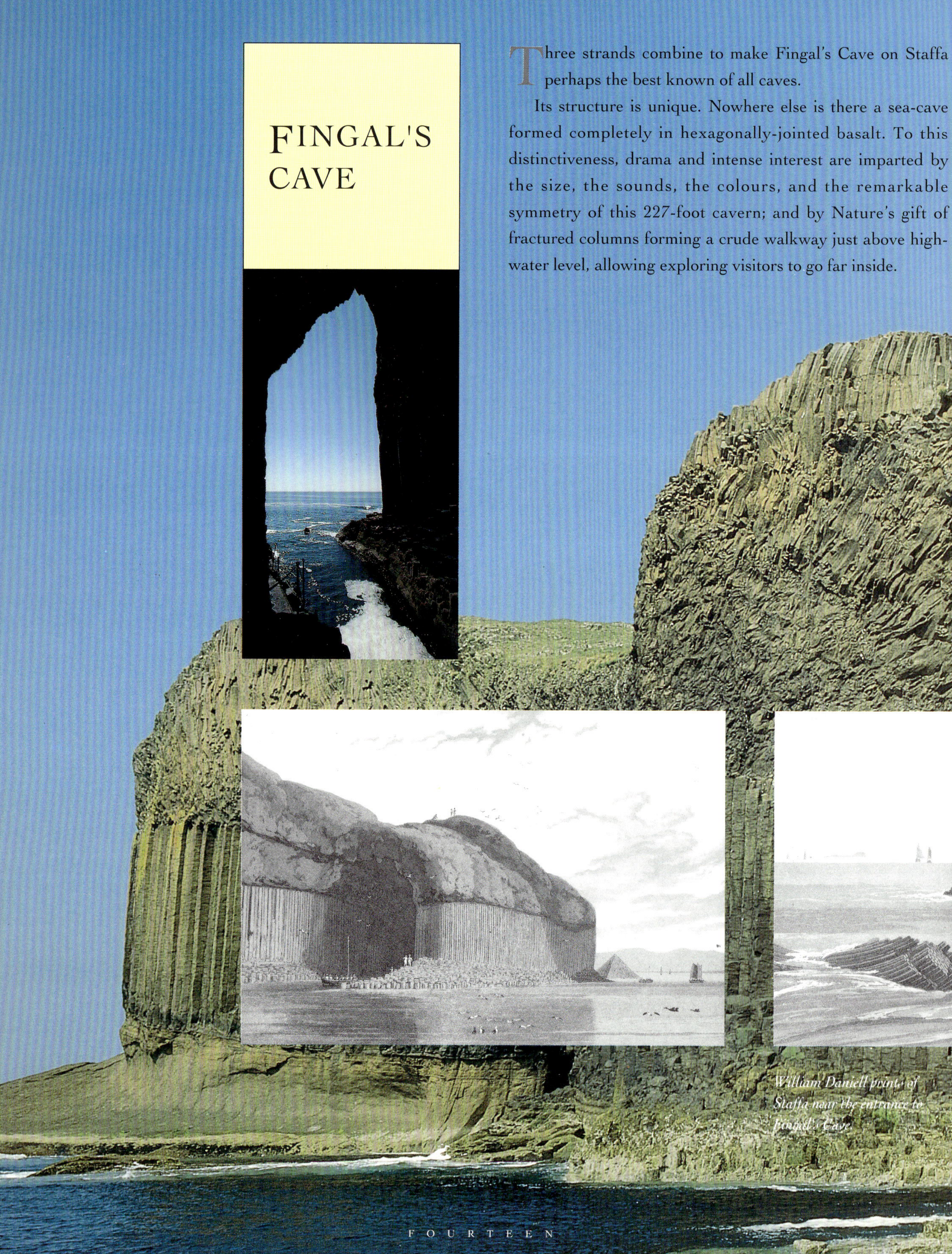

William Daniell prints of Staffa near the entrance to Fingal's Cave.

Secondly, the impact of the cave on all that enter it, and especially on those that do so alone, is likely to be remembered for life. Sir Walter Scott put it into words for us: *"... one of the most extraordinary places I ever beheld. It exceeded, in my mind, every description I had heard of it ... composed entirely of basaltic pillars as high as the roof of a cathedral, and running deep into the rock, eternally swept by a deep and swelling sea, and paved, as it were, with ruddy marble, baffles all description."*

And thirdly the evergreen popularity of Mendelssohn's "Hebrides Overture (Fingal's Cave)" provides a continuous stirring reminder of this wonder of the world.

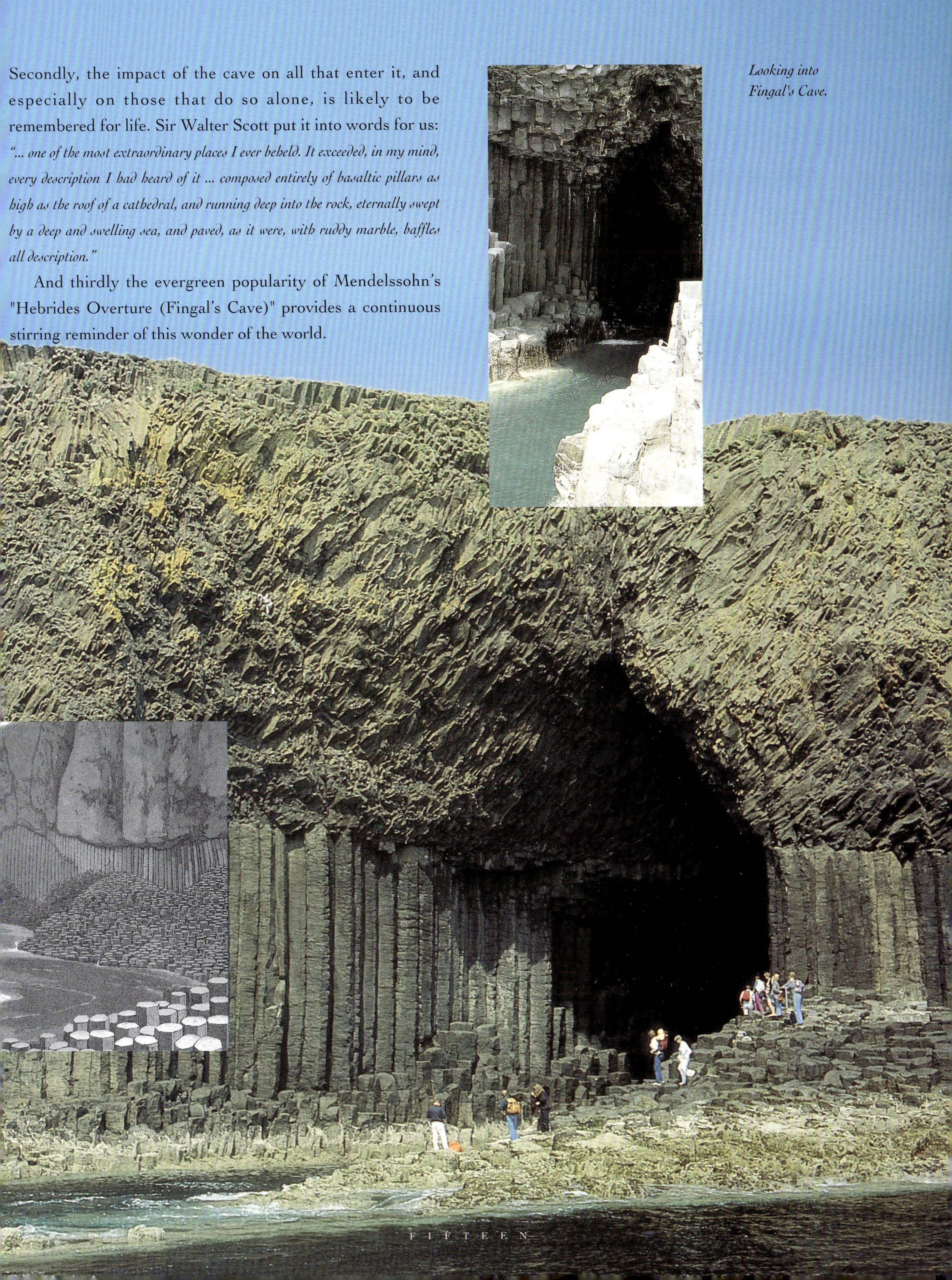

Looking into Fingal's Cave.

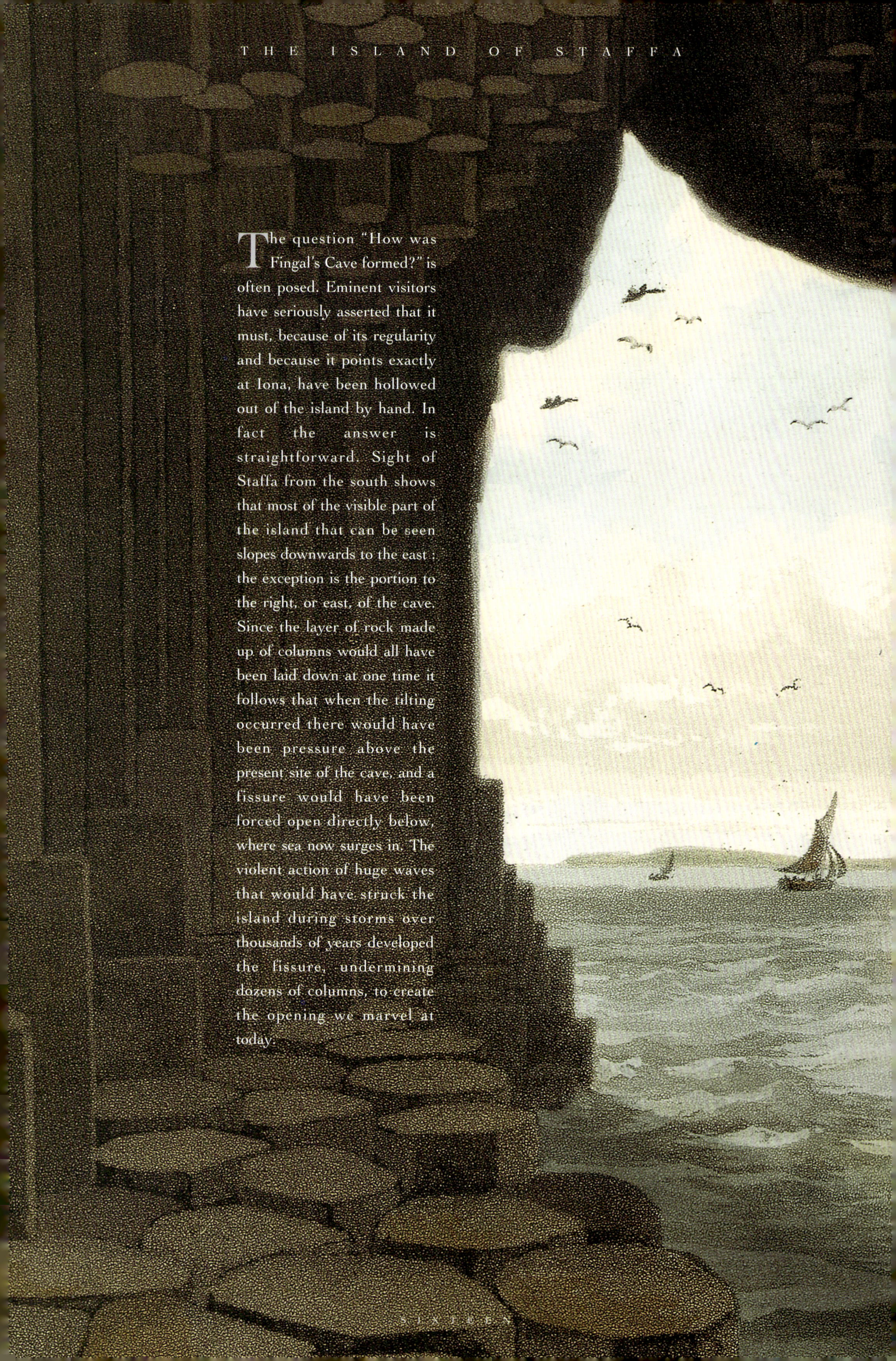

The question "How was Fingal's Cave formed?" is often posed. Eminent visitors have seriously asserted that it must, because of its regularity and because it points exactly at Iona, have been hollowed out of the island by hand. In fact the answer is straightforward. Sight of Staffa from the south shows that most of the visible part of the island that can be seen slopes downwards to the east : the exception is the portion to the right, or east, of the cave. Since the layer of rock made up of columns would all have been laid down at one time it follows that when the tilting occurred there would have been pressure above the present site of the cave, and a fissure would have been forced open directly below, where sea now surges in. The violent action of huge waves that would have struck the island during storms over thousands of years developed the fissure, undermining dozens of columns, to create the opening we marvel at today.

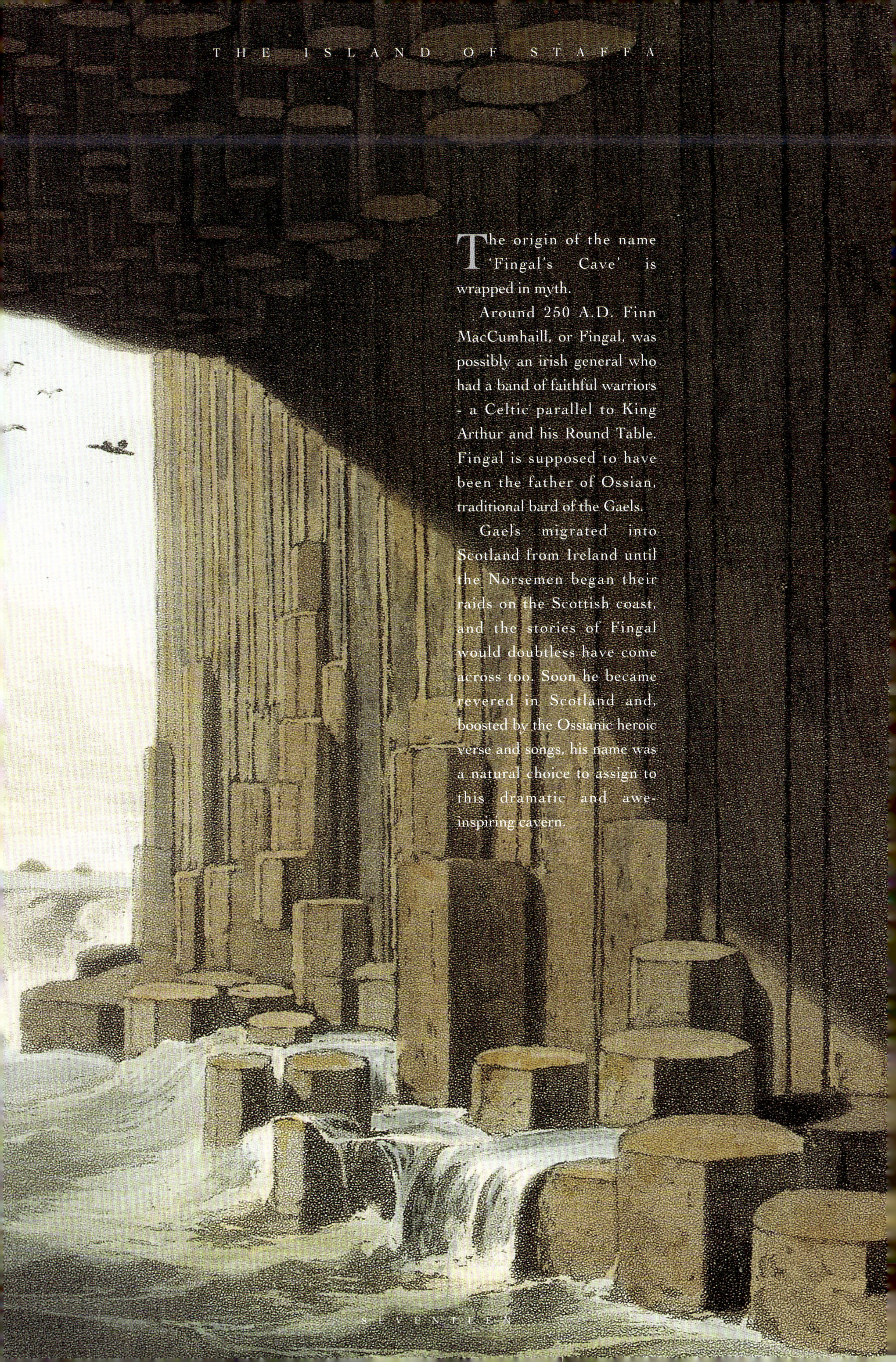

The origin of the name 'Fingal's Cave' is wrapped in myth.

Around 250 A.D. Finn MacCumhaill, or Fingal, was possibly an irish general who had a band of faithful warriors - a Celtic parallel to King Arthur and his Round Table. Fingal is supposed to have been the father of Ossian, traditional bard of the Gaels.

Gaels migrated into Scotland from Ireland until the Norsemen began their raids on the Scottish coast, and the stories of Fingal would doubtless have come across too. Soon he became revered in Scotland and, boosted by the Ossianic heroic verse and songs, his name was a natural choice to assign to this dramatic and awe-inspiring cavern.

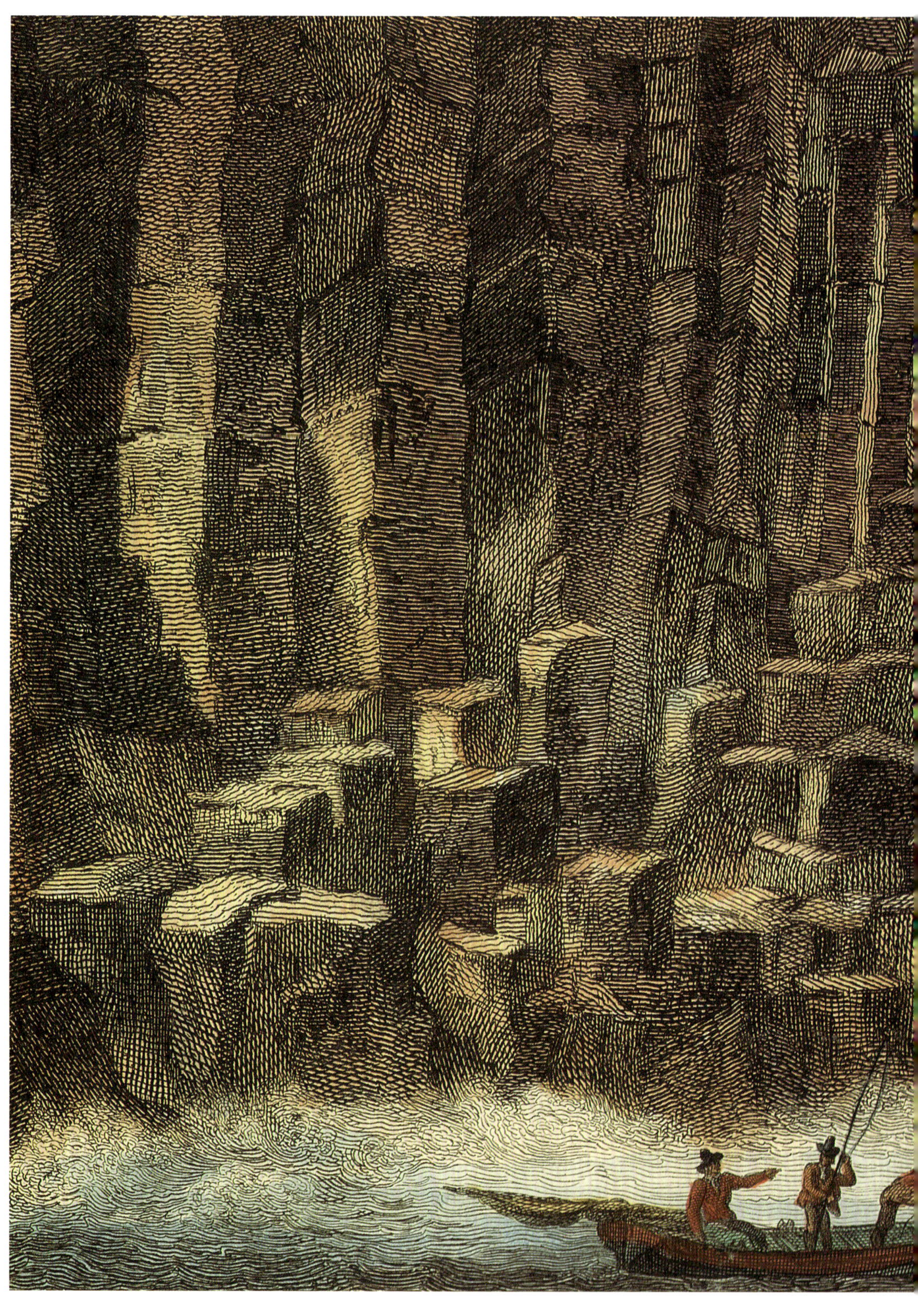

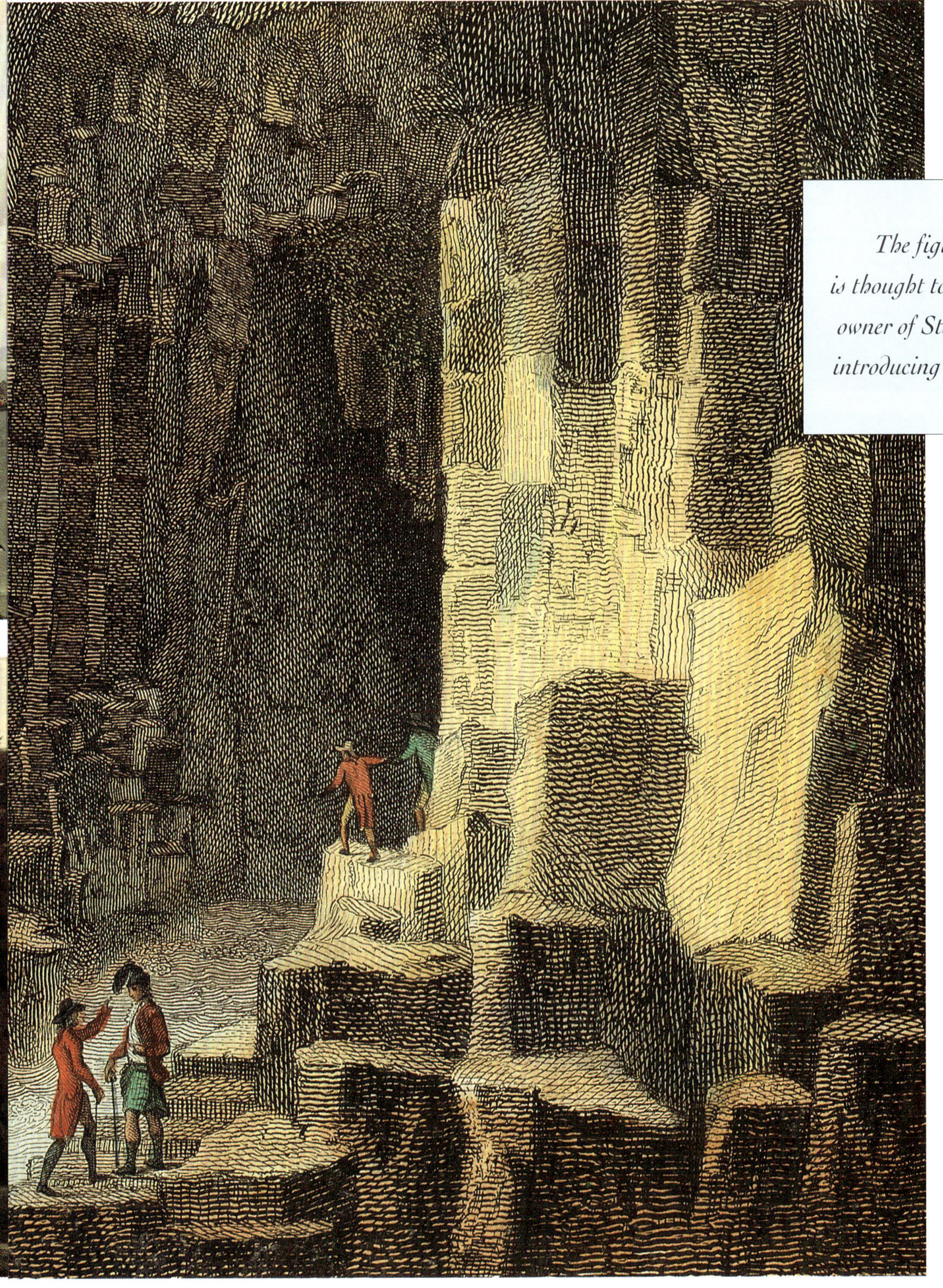

The figure with the cockade is thought to be Ranald MacDonald, owner of Staffa from 1800 to 1816, introducing guests to Fingal's Cave.

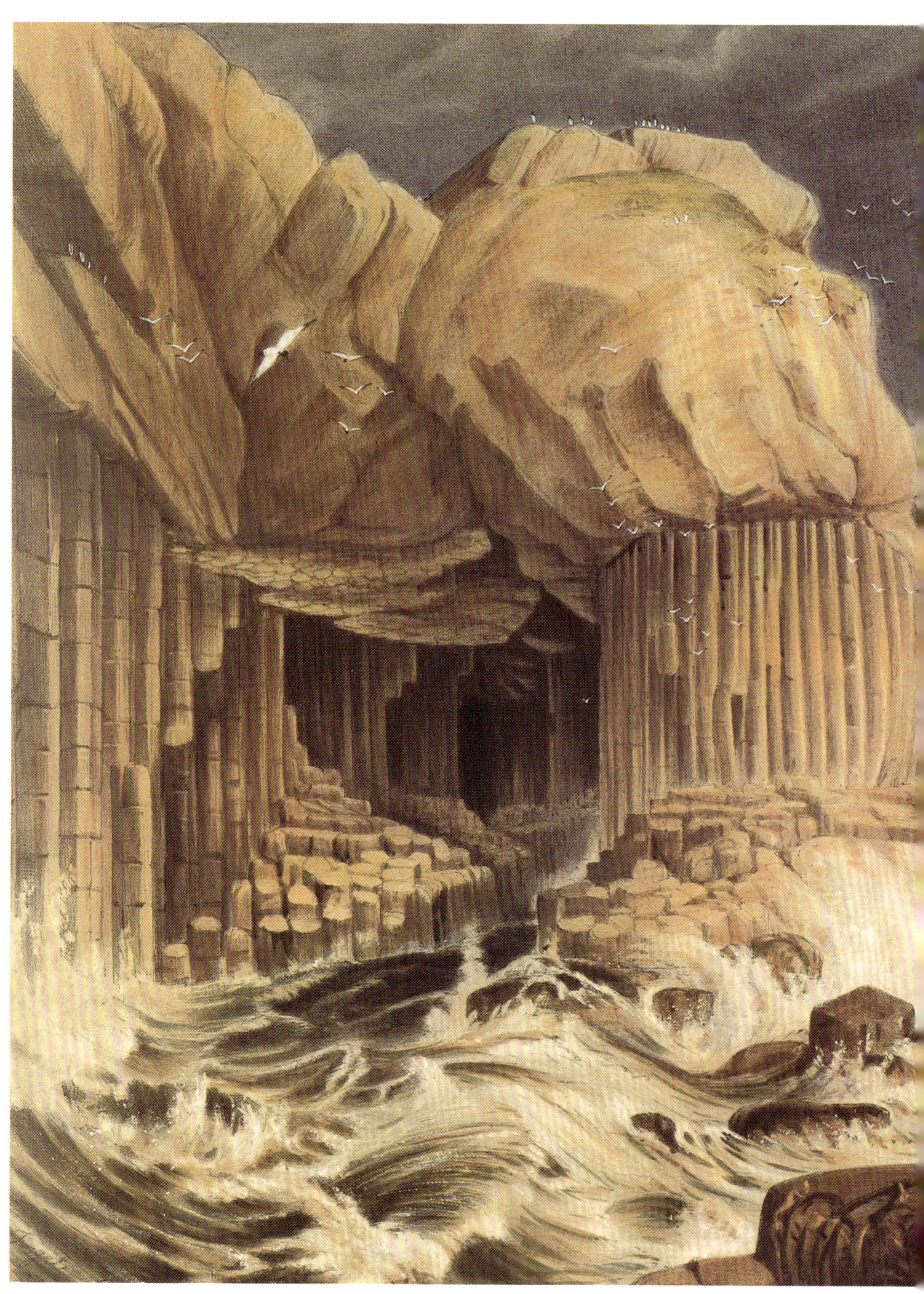

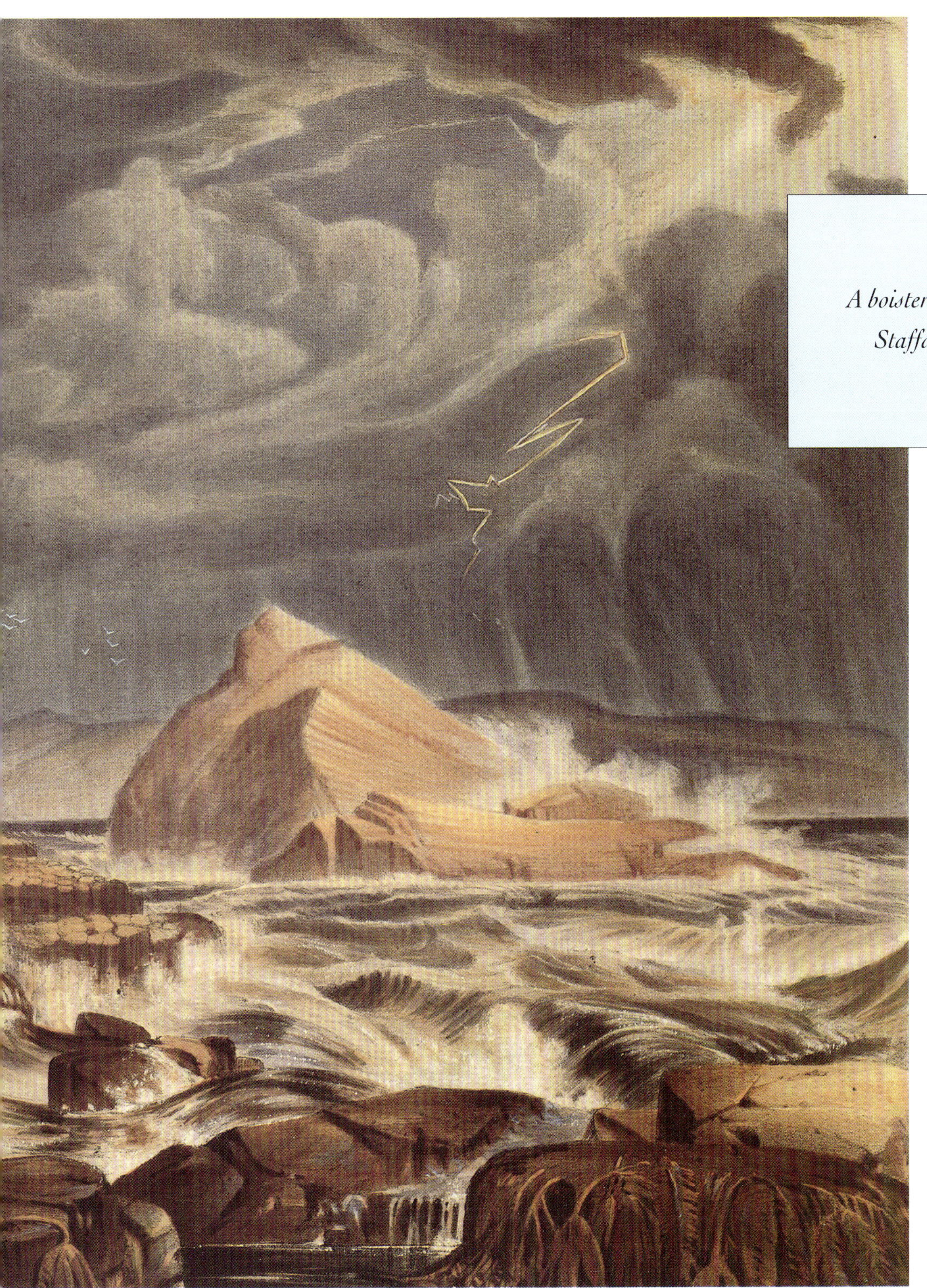

A boisterous representation of Staffa in heavy weather

THE DISCOVERY OF STAFFA

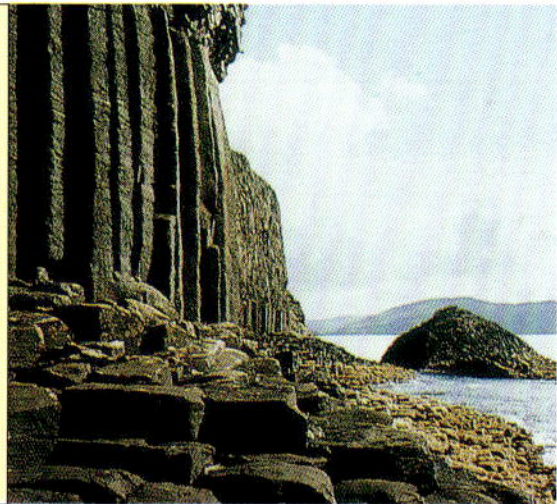

On 13th August, 1772, the illustrious scientist Joseph Banks landed on Staffa and set in train the process of publicising the island. In the November issue of The Scots Magazine that year he wrote:

"...Staffa, which is reckoned one of the greatest natural curiosities in the world, is surrounded by many pillars of different shapes such as pentagons, octagons,etc. There is a cave in this island which the natives call the Cave of Fingal: the whole sides are solid rock, and the bottom is covered with water 12 feet deep. The Giant's Causeway in Ireland, or Stonehenge in England, are but trifles when compared to this island."

This account by Banks was followed by other fuller ones, and by drawings. Before long he had generated a considerable volume of interest amongst people with enquiring minds.

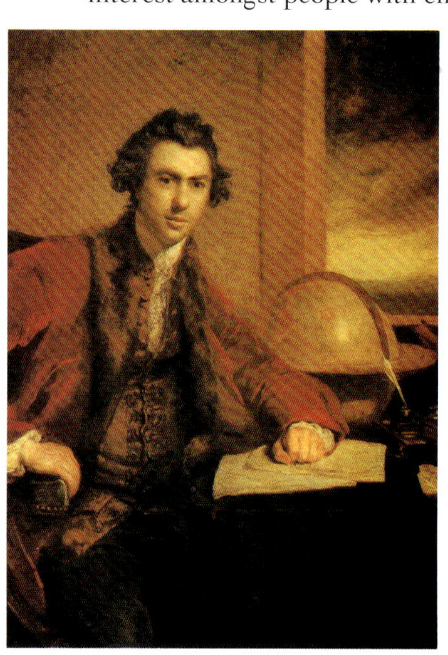

A portrait of Sir Joseph Banks when he was President of the Royal Society

At the age of 25 Banks had been selected by Captain Cook to head the team of scientists on his first round-the-world voyage from 1768 to 1771. Banks had made botany his speciality, and in the southem hemisphere he identified many previously unknown species. Botany Bay in Australia was so named by Cook in recognition of his work.

Cook invited Banks to accompany him on his second voyage, but following a disagreement about equipment and accommodation Banks decided to make studies in Iceland instead. While on his way to Iceland he was forced to shelter in the Sound of Mull. Waiting for the weather to improve, he accepted an invitation to be entertained ashore. At the merry-making he was introduced to an Englishman, a Mr Leach, who told Banks that nine leagues away lay an island with pillars of rock, as on the Giant's Causeway, where no one even in the Highlands had ever been. The

island proved to be Staffa. In a state of great excitement, he inspected it the next day.

In 1778 Banks was elected President of the Royal Society, becoming "Sir Joseph" when he was knighted in 1781. He retained the presidency of the Society until his death in 1820, holding the post for an unsurpassed 42 years.

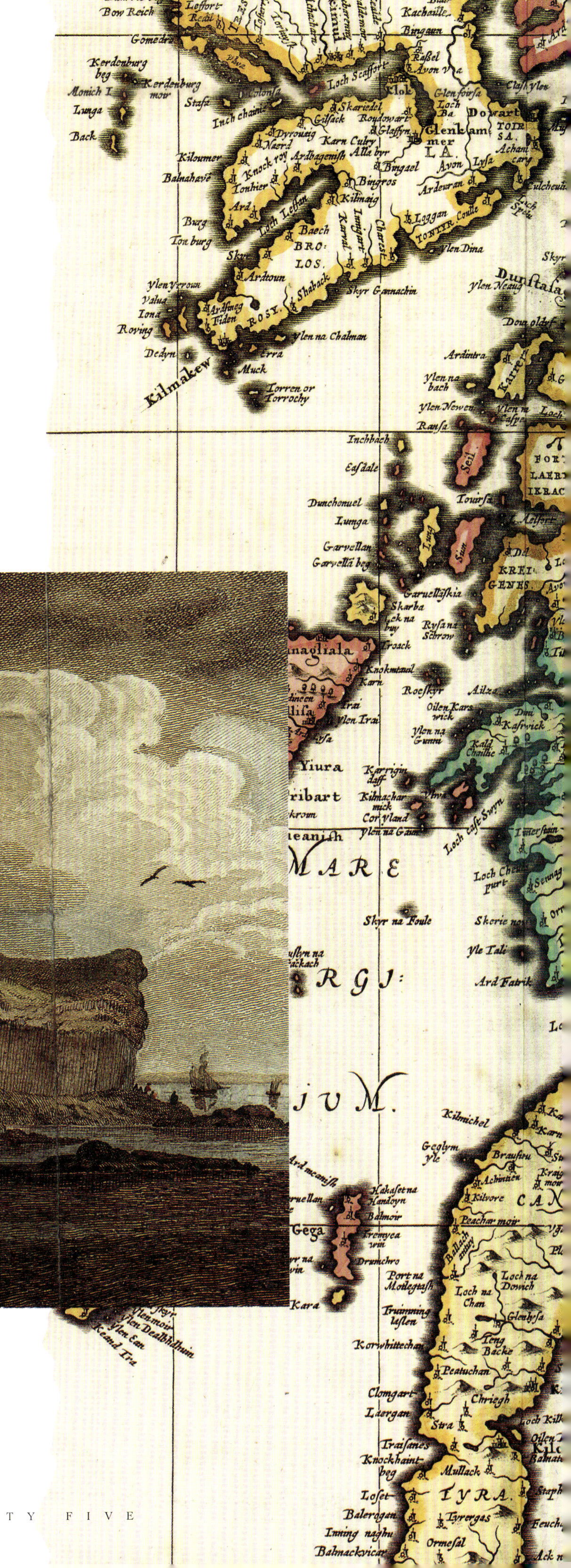

An 18th century engraving of Staffa and contemporary vessels of various kinds

INHABITANTS

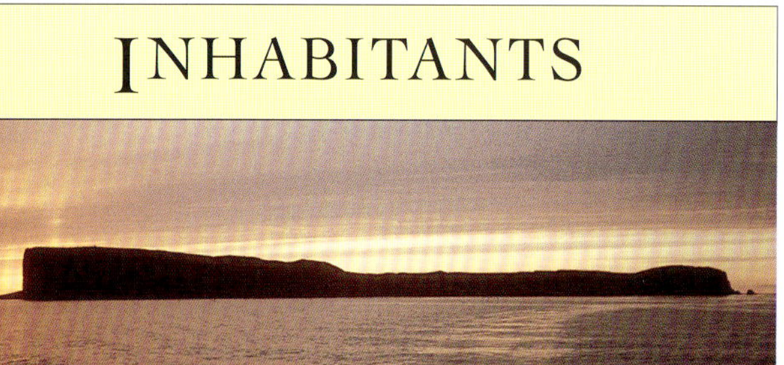

Until about 200 years ago people used to live on Staffa. When Banks landed in 1772 he found the island occupied by a solitary "peasant who attends some cattle that pasture there".

Faujas, the French geologist, visiting Staffa in 1784 found the population to be 16, living in two huts "constructed of unhewn blocks of basalt roofed over with sods. There were eight cows, one bull, twelve sheep, two horses, one pig, two dogs, one cock and eight hens".

When Professor T.Garner went to Staffa in 1798 he also found two huts, and commented that "the manner of life is extremely simple, food consisting chiefly of milk and potatoes with, now and then, a little fish". That was the final year in which the island was lived on continuously. Thereafter, for the following decade, herdsmen and their families resided on Staffa from spring to autumn; and then habitation came to an end.

Animals, however, have gone on spending time on Staffa. A visitor in 1826 reported finding cows, horses and sheep "without a guardian and without shelter". Sheep are still grazed on the island.

From the air the lazy-beds in which residents grew the potatoes necessary for their survival can be clearly seen. Surprisingly, in view of the harsh weather, oats also grew moderately well. Most of the surface of the island was cultivated at some time; though latterly some was stripped of turfs to burn, setting back the possibility of growing crops.

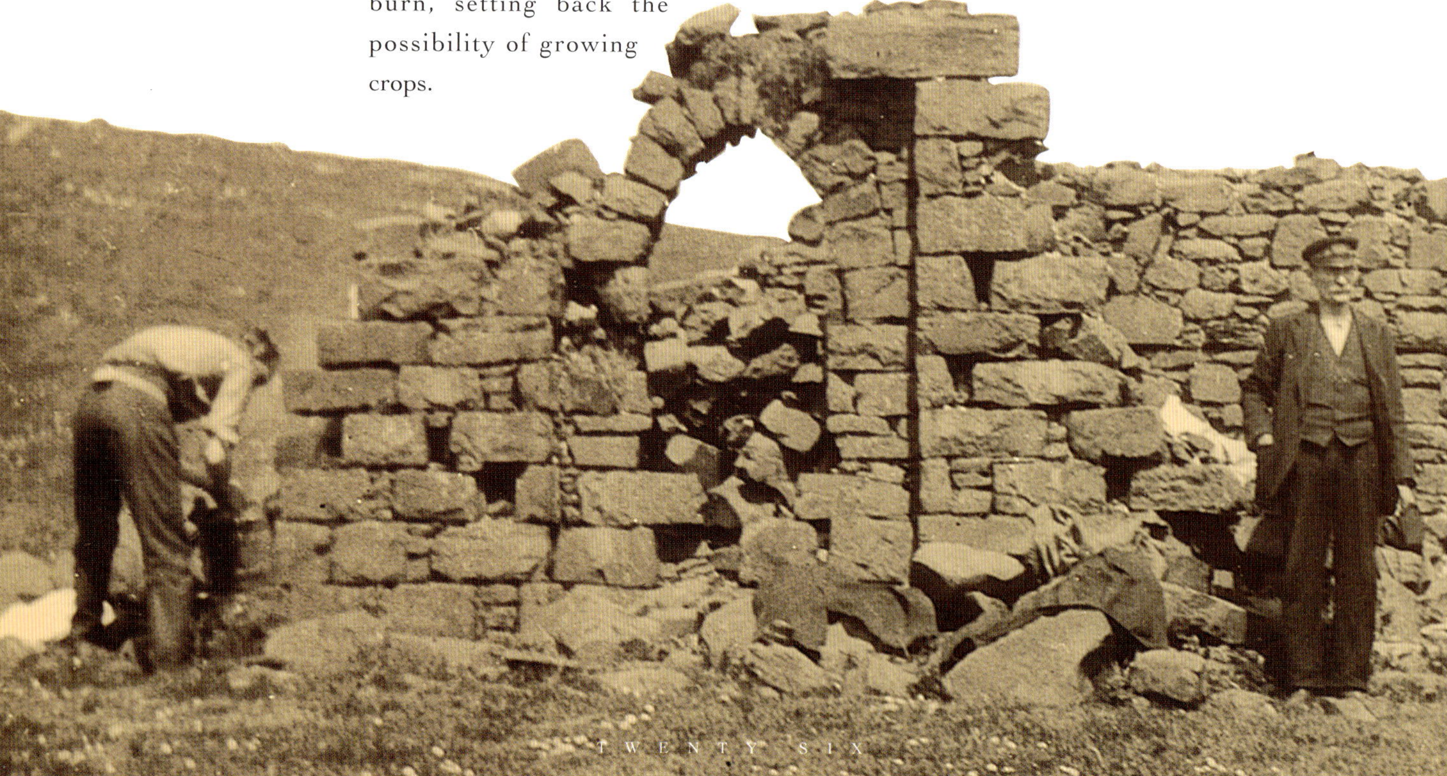

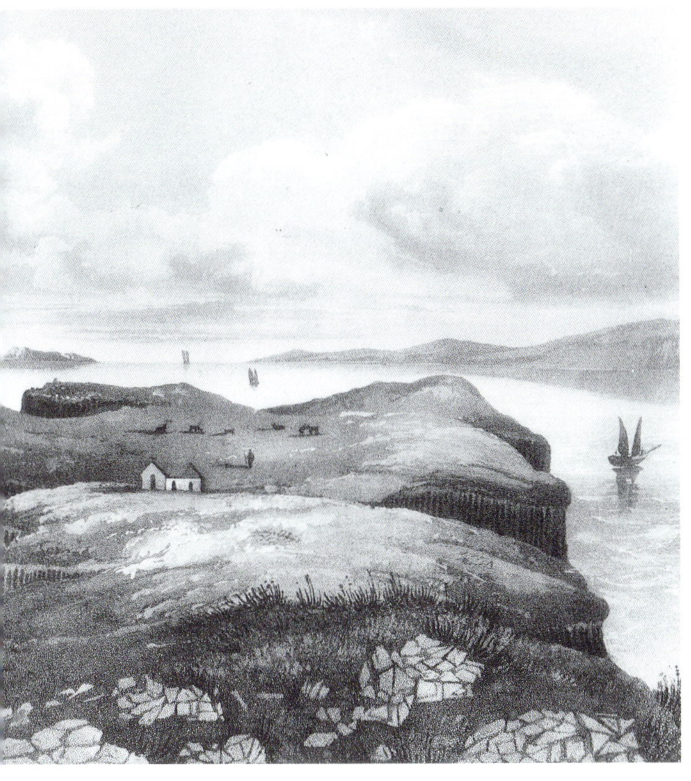

The stone ruin, visible today, which was long believed to be the remains of a mediaeval chapel or hermit's cell, has presented a riddle.

Its presence was not noted by any visitor before 1830, the year in which Pancoucke included the roofless building in his painting of Staffa's plateau. Now it is widely assumed that the structure was a folly erected in the 1820s. Over the years, the building, in various stages of collapse, has provided visitors with shelter from the weather.

Above: Pancoucke's sketch of the plateau of Staffa, including the only known representation of the building before it collapsed.

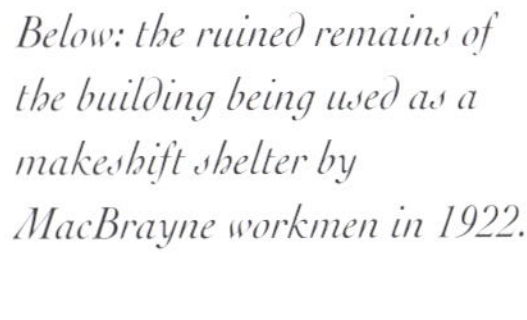

Below: the ruined remains of the building being used as a makeshift shelter by MacBrayne workmen in 1922.

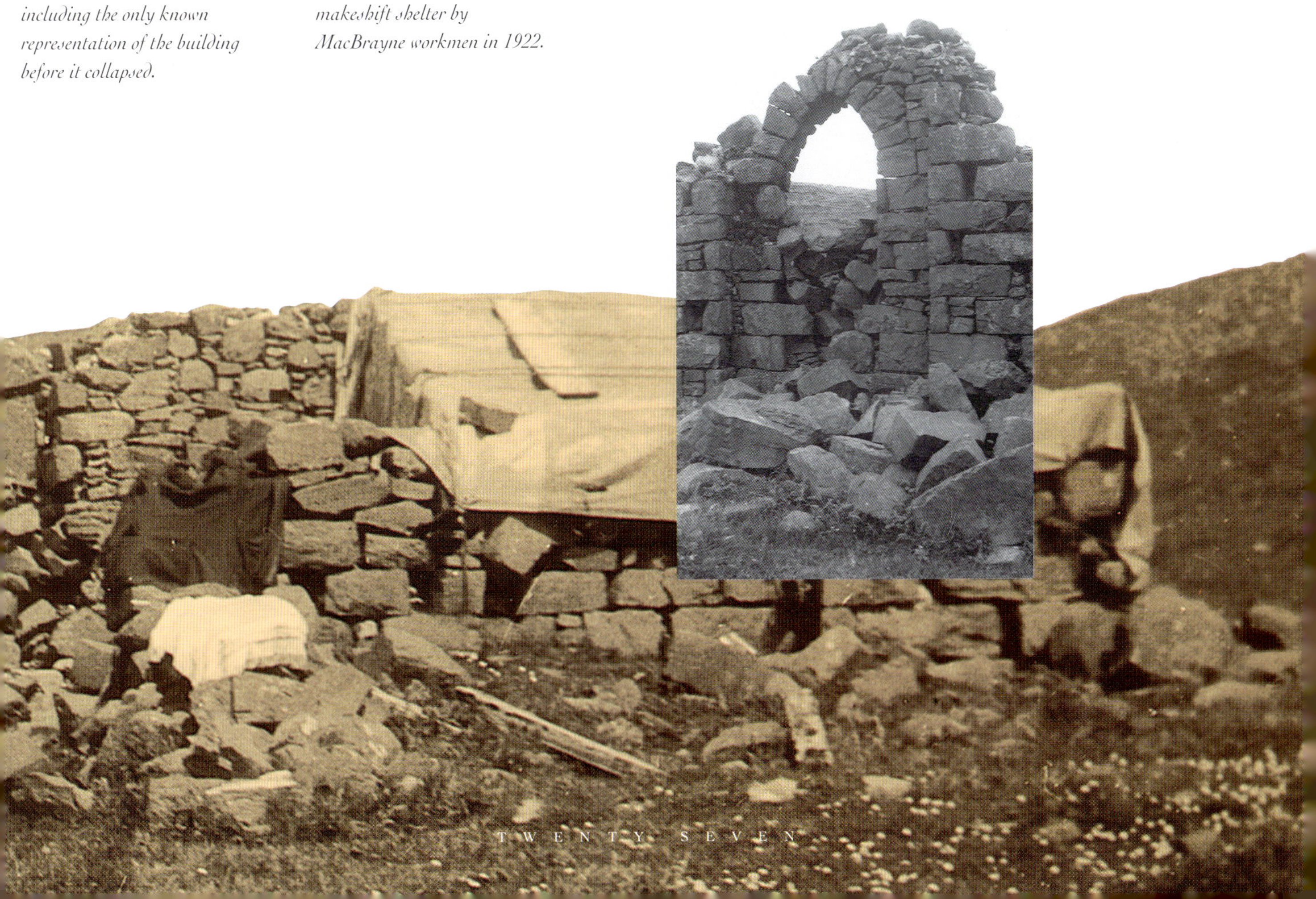

NOTABLE VISITORS TO STAFFA

On 19th August, 1847, **Queen Victoria** accompanied by Prince Albert and the young Prince of Wales and the Princess Royal sailed to Staffa in the royal yacht. In her *Leaves from the Journal of our Life in the Highlands* she described the occasion.

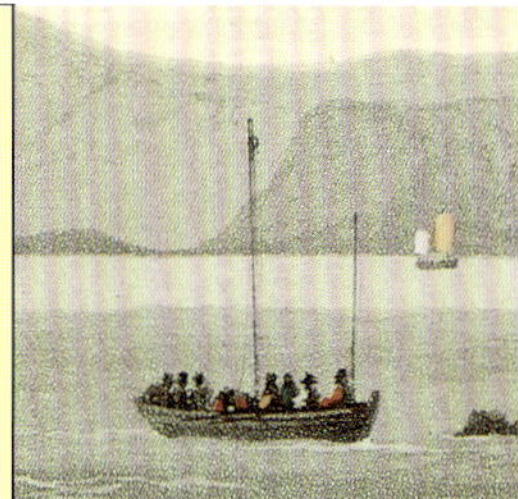

At three we anchored close before Staffa, and immediately got into the barge with Charles, the children and the rest of our people, and rowed towards the cave. As we rounded the point, the wonderful basaltic formation came into sight. The appearance it presents is most extraordinary; and when we turned the corner to go into the renowned Fingal's Cave, the effect was splendid, like a great entrance into a vaulted hall: it looked almost awful as we entered and the barge heaved up and down on the swell of the sea. It is very high, but not longer than 227 feet, and narrower than I expected, being only 40 feet wide. The sea is immensely deep in the cave. The rocks, under water, were all colours - pink, blue, and green - which had a most beautiful and varied effect.

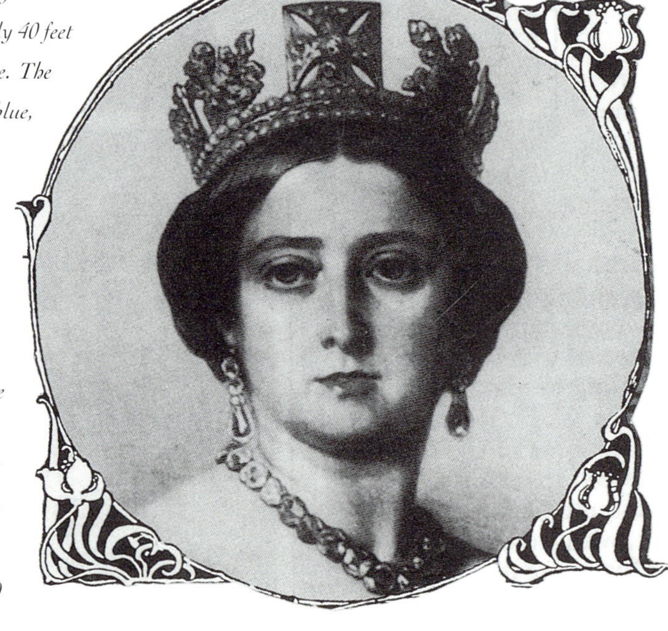

It was the first time the British standard with a Queen of Great Britain, and her husband and children, had ever entered Fingal's Cave, and the men gave three cheers, which sounded very impressive there. We backed out, and then went a little further to look at the other cave, not of basaltic formation, and at the point called the Herdsman. The swell was beginning to get up, and perhaps an hour later we could not have gone in.

Queen Victoria was just one of a large number of celebrities to go to Staffa, and record their impressions of it, in the hundred years or so after Sir Joseph Banks brought its amazing features to the attention of the public.

Dr **Samuel Johnson** was already planning his excursion to Scotland, made with James Boswell in 1773, when news of Banks' account of finding Staffa reached him; and he may well have decided to try and include an inspection of the island in his itinerary.

However he was too late in the year, and luck was against him. He reached Mull on 14th October, staying with Sir Alexander MacLean on Inchkenneth. In his *A Tour to the Hebrides with Samuel Johnson, LL.D., in 1773* Boswell says *"We saw the island of Staffa at no very great distance, but could not land on it, the surge was so high on its rocky coast."*

Dr Samuel Johnson on his tour of the Highlands in 1773.

In 1829, on 7th August, **Felix Mendelssohn** had more success, although suffering more discomfort. With his friend Klingemann, Mendelssohn set out on the newly introduced paddle steamer service to sail round Mull calling at Iona and Staffa, returning down the Sound of Mull to Oban. The day was wild and all the passengers were ill. Klingemann tells of the arrival at Staffa:

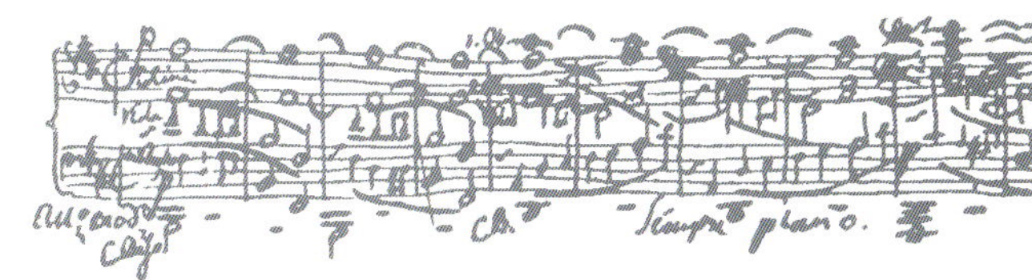

Part of Mendelssohn's original score for his Hebrides Overture.

We were put out into boats and lifted by the hissing sea up the pillar stumps to the celebrated Fingal's Cave. A greener roar of waves surely never rushed into a stranger cavern - its many pillars making it look like the inside of an immense organ, black and resounding, and absolutely without purpose, and quite alone, the wide grey sea within and without.

Conditions were so bad that the little craft had only reached Tobermory by nightfall, and Mendelssohn can hardly have enjoyed seeing Fingal's Cave since he was so seasick. However the visit to Staffa, and the sight and sound of the Atlantic swell tumbling into the Cave, made a profound impression on him. The theme in the illustration, which he later developed into the ever-popular Hebrides Overture, occurred to him immediately. He was just 20 years old.

Felix Mendelssohn as a young man.

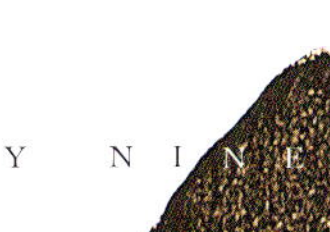

The following year, 1830, **J.M.W.Turner**, probably Britain's greatest painter, and certainly the most versatile, made the journey to Staffa. In fulfilling a commission from Sir Walter Scott to provide twenty-four drawings to illustrate *The Lord of the Isles* Turner needed to record an impression of Fingal's Cave. His imaginative, almost surrealistic, sketch which aroused mixed feelings is reproduced here. He also created a major oil painting titled 'Staffa, Fingal's Cave' which was exhibited in the Royal Academy in 1832 and was generally thought to be more successful. Sadly, apart from a short period in the middle of this century when it belonged to Lord Astor and hung in Hever Castle, the work has always had its home in U.S.A.

Turner's impression of Fingal's Cave.

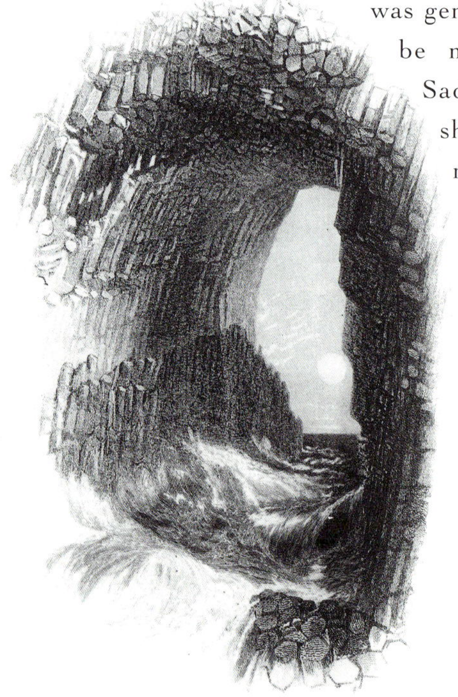

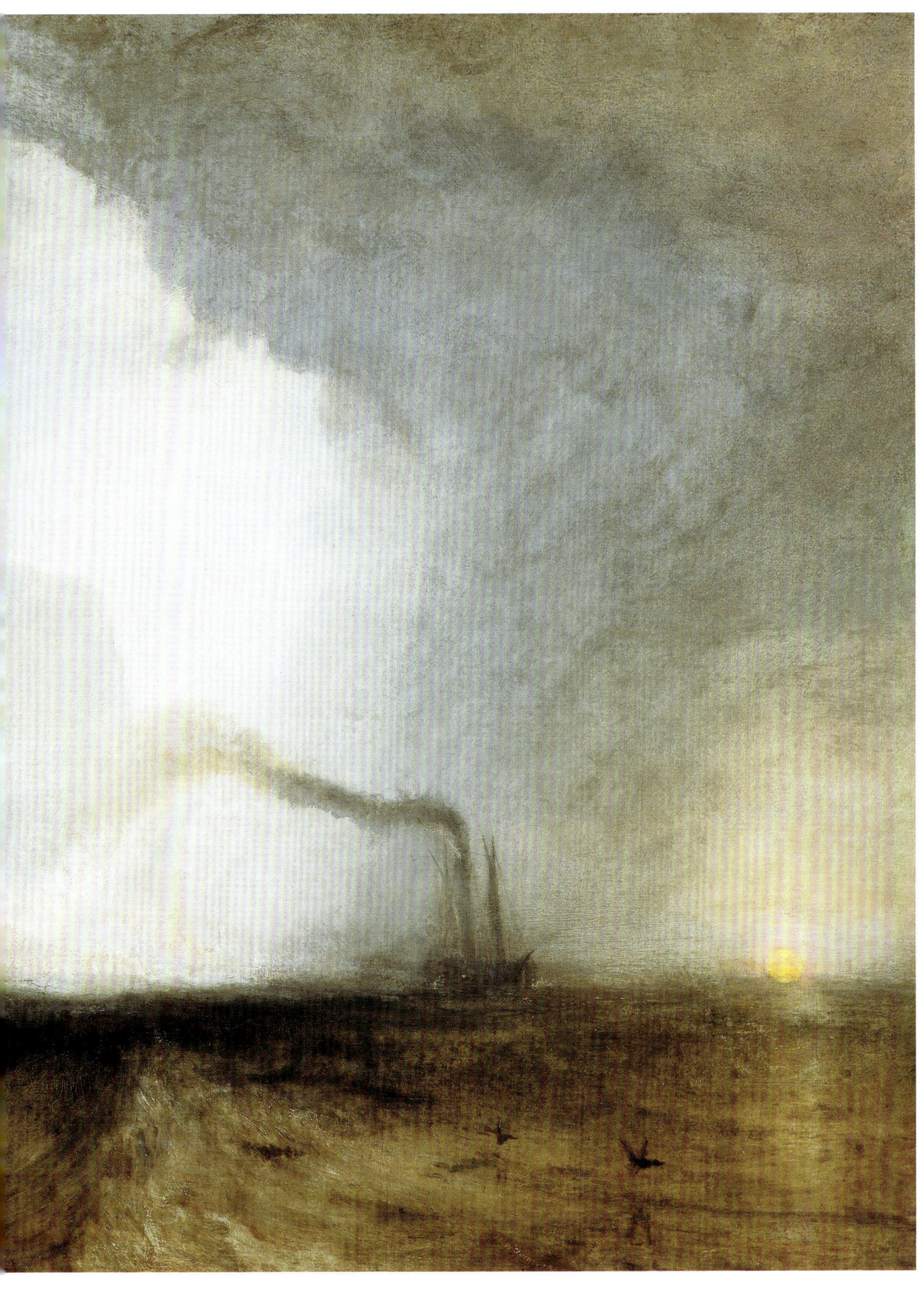

'Staffa, Fingal's Cave' painted by Turner in 1831. When challenged on its vagueness Turner replied "Indistinctness is my forte."

Sir Walter Scott was a friend of Ranald MacDonald who owned the Ulva estate, including Staffa, from 1800 until 1816. Scott made two trips to Staffa - in 1810 and 1814 - each time residing with MacDonald. He found Fingal's Cave *"as being 'dont on parle en histoire', one of the few 'lions' which completely maintain an extended reputation."* In *The Lord of the Isles* he wrote:

The shores of Mull on the eastward lay,
And Ulva dark and Colonsay,
And all the group of islets gay
That guard famed Staffa round.

Then all unknown its columns rose,
Where dark and undisturbed repose
The cormorant had found,
And the shy seal had quiet home,
and weltered in that wondrous dome,
Where Nature herself, it seemed, would raise
A Minster to her Maker's praise!

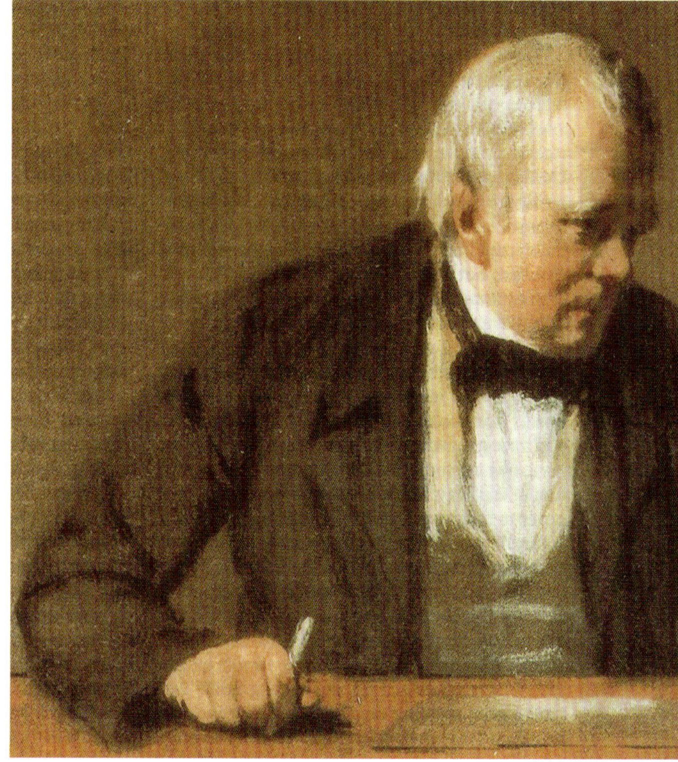

Not for a meaner use ascend
Her columns, or her arches bend;
Nor of a theme less solemn tells
That mighty surge that ebbs and swells
And still between each awful pause
From the high vault an answer draws,
In varied tone prolong'd and high,
That mocks the organ's melody.

Nor doth its entrance front in vain
To old Iona's holy fane,
That Nature's voice might seem to say,
Well hast thou done, frail child of clay,
Thy humble powers that stately shrine
Task'd high and hard - but witness mine!

These final six lines allude to the strange fact that Iona and its abbey can be seen on a good day from the back of Fingal's Cave.

The three English poets **John Keats, William Wordsworth,** and **Alfred Lord Tennyson** each made the journey to Staffa during the nineteenth century. Although there is no record of the effect the island had on Tennyson, the other two wrote graphically about it. Wordsworth's verse, in part, runs:

O, for those motions only that invite
The Ghost of Fingal to his tuneful cave
By the breeze entered, and wave after wave
Softly embosoming the timid light!

The pillared vestibule,
Expanding yet precise, the roof embowed,
Might seem destined to humble man, when proud
Of his best workmanship by plan and tool.
Down-bearing with his while Atlantic weight
Of tide and tempest on the structure's base,
And flashing to that structure's topmost height,
Ocean has proved its strength, and of its grace
In calm is conscious, finding for its freight
Of softest music some responsive place.

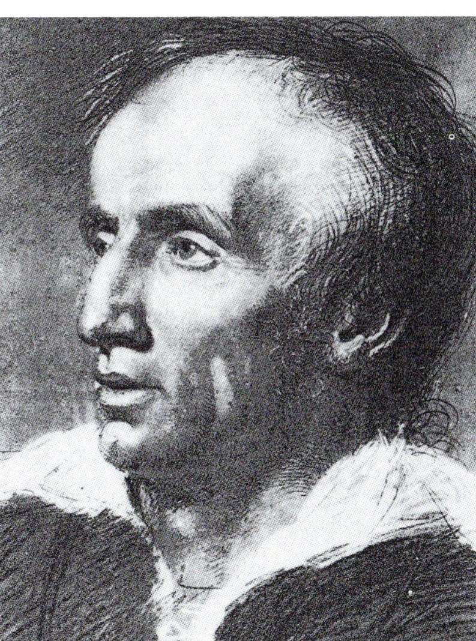

William Wordsworth

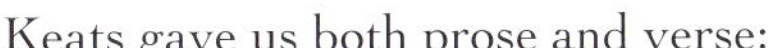

Keats gave us both prose and verse:

Suppose, now, the giants who came down to the daughters of men had taken a whole mass of these columns and bound them together like bunches of matches,and then with immense axes had made a cavern in the body of these columns. Such is Fingal's Cave, except that the sea has done the work of excavation and is continually dashing there. The colour of the columns is a sort of black, with a lurking gloom of purple therein. For solemnity and grandeur it far surpasses the finest cathedral.

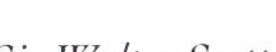

Sir Walter Scott

This was archectur'd thus
By the great Oceanus -
Here his mighty waters play
Hollow organs all the day;
Here, by turns, his dolphins all,
Finny palmers, great and small,
Come and pay devotion due,
Each a mouth of pearls must strew.

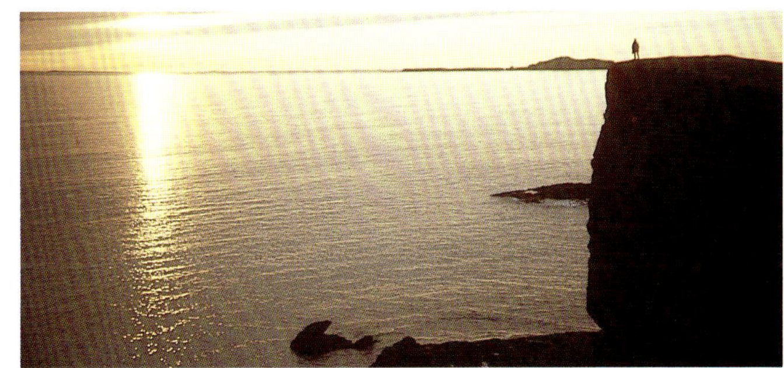

Another formidable literary figure, **Jules Verne**, called at Staffa in 1859. Some years later he published *Le Rayon Vert*, or 'The Green Ray', a romantic book in which the climax of the story takes place on the island. From its western cliffs the characters in the story witnessed that rare phenomenon, the green ray or flash, which occurs, if atmospheric conditions are right, at the moment when the sun finally disappears below the horizon formed by the sea.

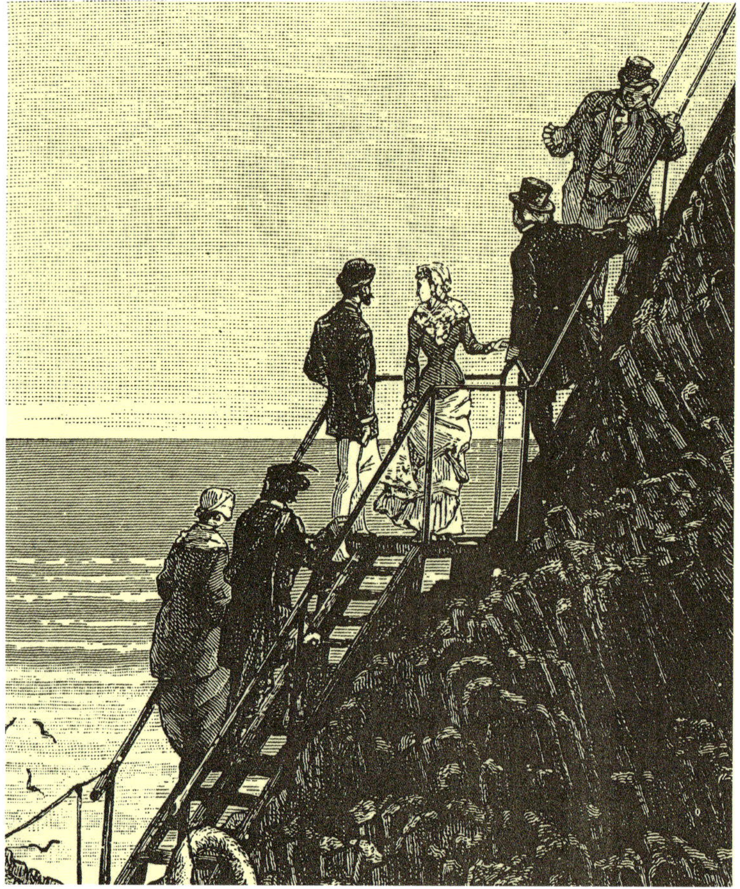

A drawing of the stairway at Clamshell Cave taken from the Jules Verne's 'The Green Ray'.

Robert Louis Stevenson had family connections with the island of Erraid adjacent to Iona. His father and uncle were responsible for the construction of the Dubh Artach lighthouse 15 miles south-west of Iona, and they quarried the granite needed on Erraid. Later R.L.Stevenson made Erraid the scene of the shipwreck in his *Kidnapped*. He landed on Staffa more than once when travelling to and from Oban, and knew the island well.

OWNERS OF STAFFA

The National Trust for Scotland is alleged to be only the ninth owner of Staffa. For many years, starting long before any records were kept, the MacQuarrie family owned the Ulva estate which included Staffa.

The estate was sold in 1777, five years after Banks discovered Staffa, and it then changed hands rapidly twice more before being bought in 1785 by Colin MacDonald of Boisdale (who, incidentally, is great-great-great-grandfather of the author). Colin was the son of Alexander MacDonald of Boisdale who found himself in trouble with the authorities in London for helping the Prince escape to France when he was on the run in the Western Isles following the battle of Culloden in 1746.

Opposite: Part of the Lyon Court's charter granting Arms to Staffa.

In 1800, when Colin died, the estate passed to the eldest son by his second marriage, the 23-year-old Ranald MacDonald. He became a friend of Sir Walter Scott, hosting him on Ulva in flamboyant style in 1810 and 1814 when they both visited Staffa. Money troubles forced Ranald in 1816 to sell Staffa into the hands of trustees where it remained for 150 years.

Ranald MacDonald

The island was finally bought by a retired army padre, Gerald Newell, and sold by him to the author in 1972. In 1978 he sold it to Mr Lang whose family had a particular interest in the birdlife of Staffa : shortly afterwards it was back on the market, to be bought by Mr Jock Elliott Jr. formerly chairman of Ogilvy & Mather. With great generosity he gave Staffa to the National Trust for Scotland in 1986 to commemorate his wife's 60th birthday.

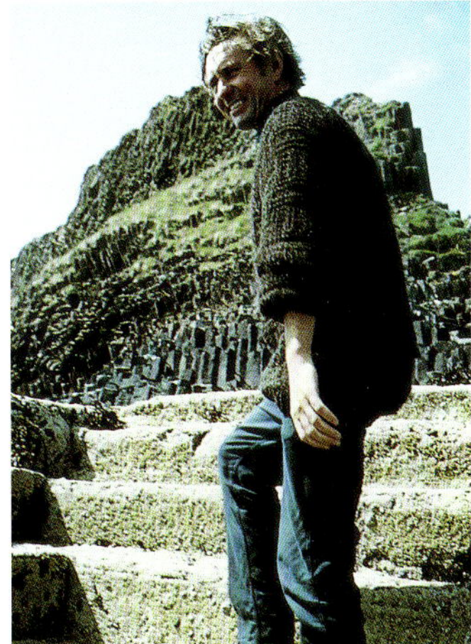

The author stepping ashore on Staffa, for the first time, in 1972.

THE NATURAL HISTORY OF STAFFA

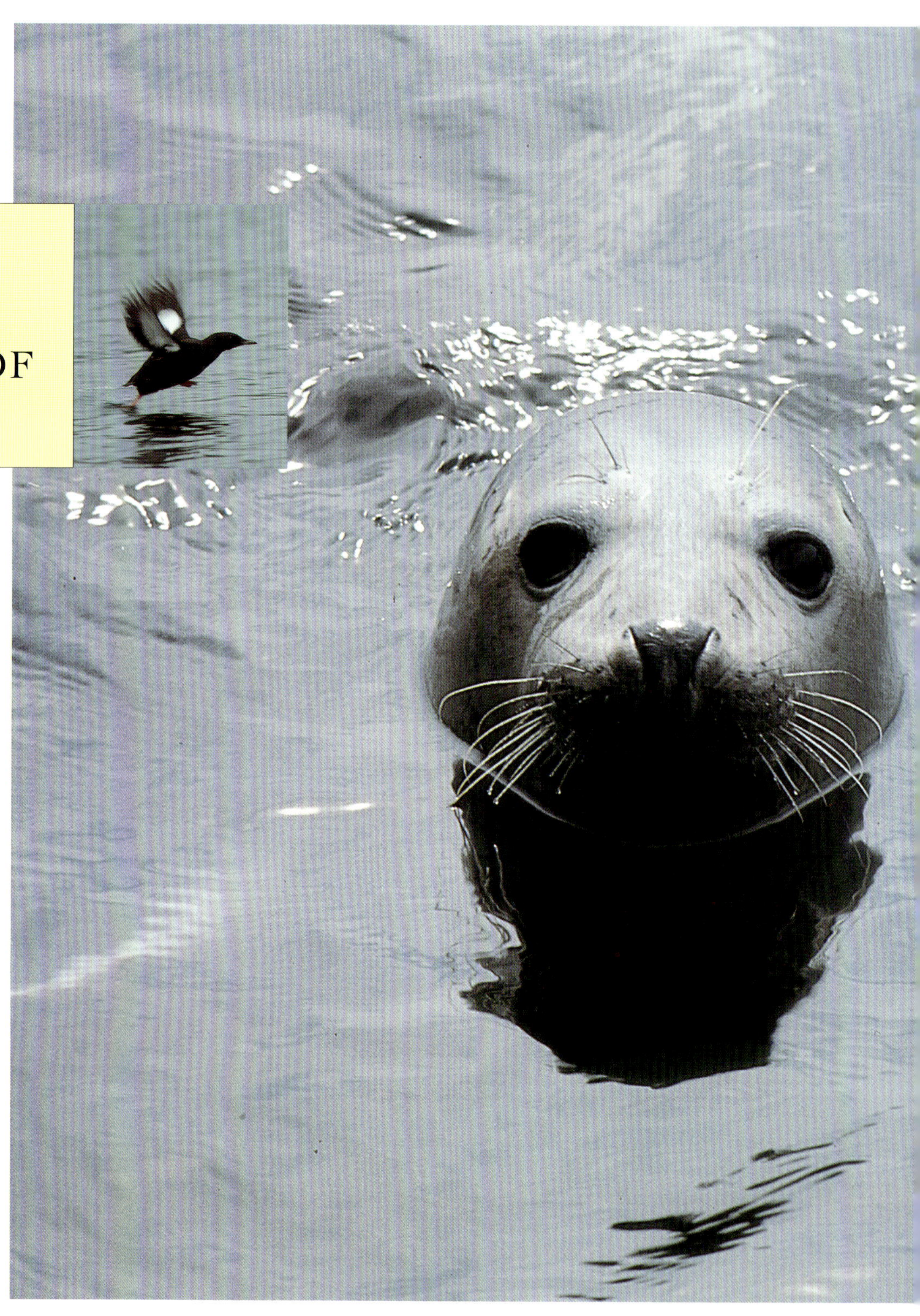

Above right: Black Guillemot

Seals are often in the water close to Staffa.

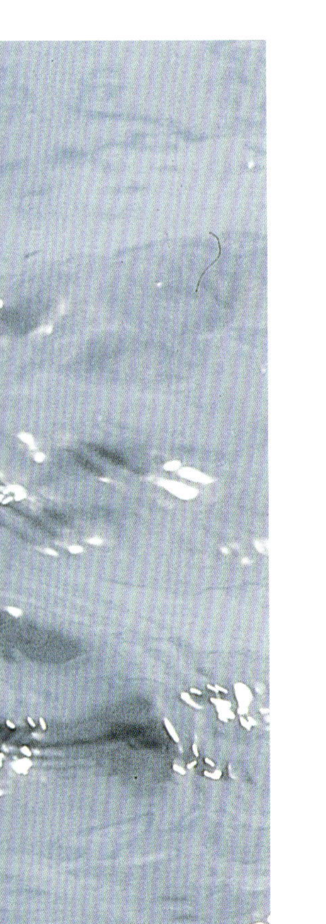

The colonies of sea-birds that breed on Staffa, and those that simply pause there to rest and feed, add greatly to the interest of a visit. Amongst the most abundant and most dependable are puffins, cormorants and shags, fulmars, and great black-backed gulls; others, such as razorbills, are less regular.

Puffins delight everyone with their antics and the difficulty they seem to have in becoming airborne. Late in August, when the juveniles have developed enough to leave their burrows and fly strongly, all the puffins head out into the Atlantic for the winter.

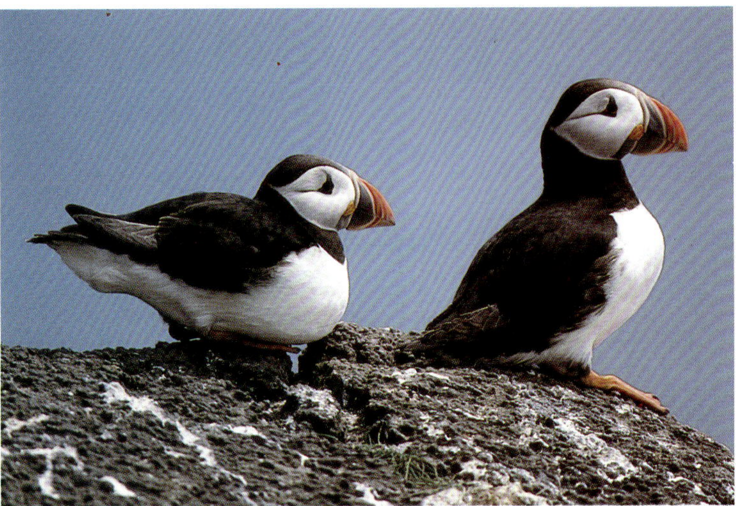

Puffins at Staffa.

The cormorants are engaging, too. They stand for ages, perfectly still, on the rocks and skerries just off Staffa facing into the wind with their wings extended. They are unexpectedly tame: one couple in particular which nests near the top of Clamshell Cave contemptuously ignores all human activity.

Ashore the gulls command the most attention. The great black-backs nest in the area Meall nam Faoleann (The Hill of the Gulls) marked on the map. They are big and raucous, and a threat to any small animals such as new-born lambs.

In addition to the sea-birds rock pipits, starlings, wheatears and larks sometimes breed on Staffa.

In the sea around the island seals are often in evidence; and fishermen catch mackerel, salmon and lobsters close by.

Thrift

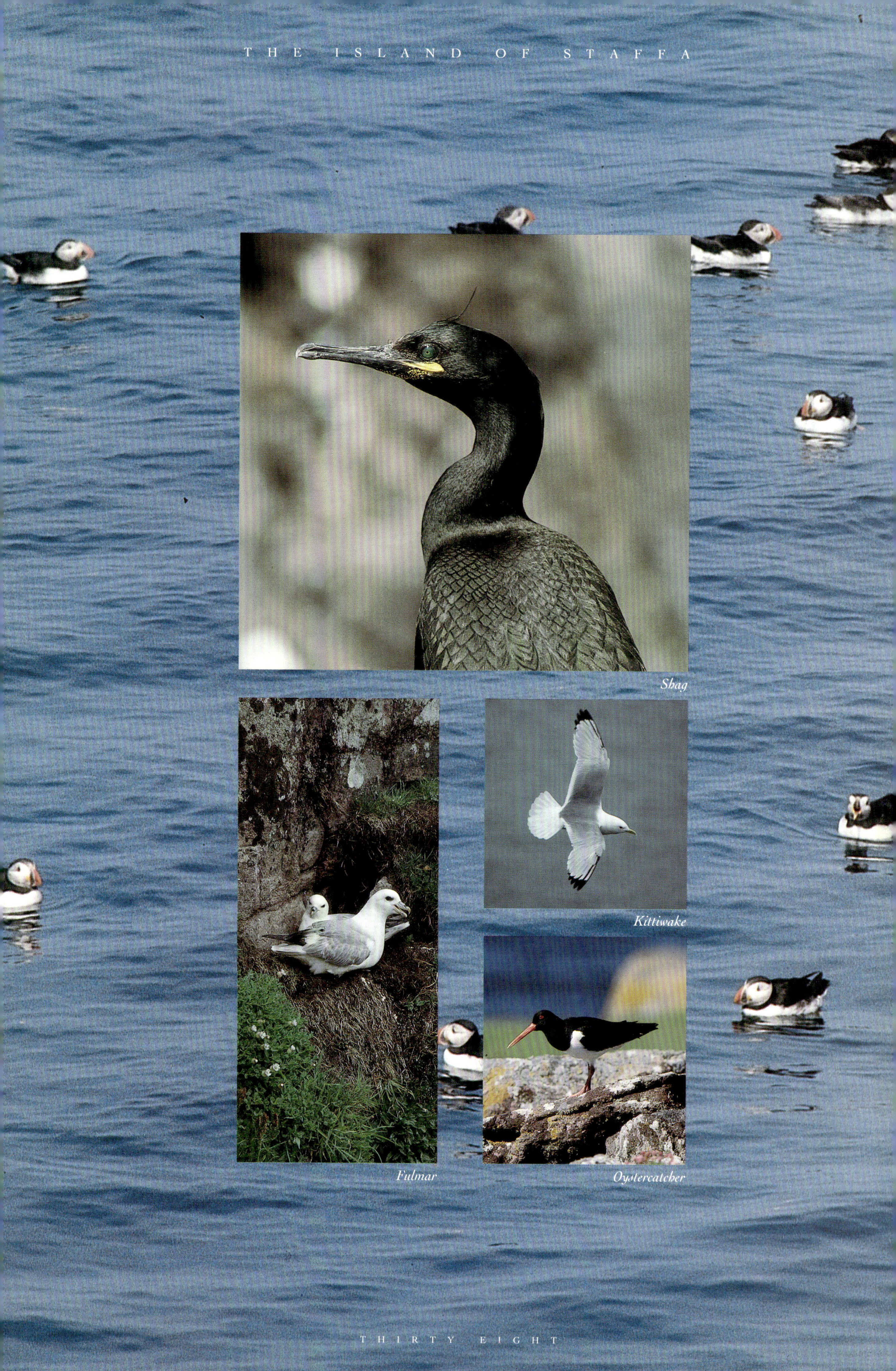

Shag

Kittiwake

Fulmar

Oystercatcher

The diverse pattern of soil types on Staffa, arising from the basaltic lavas, allows a great range of plant communities to flourish. The 150 different higher plants constitute an unusually rich flora for so small an island.

Despite this wealth of plant life, there is almost no bracken; and no heather, trees or shrubs. However, plentiful colour is provided by the sea campion, thrift, buttercup, and by the rich lichens on the south-facing colonnade near the major caves.

Thus, while the exceptional geological features are recognised as being of outstanding importance, the whole island's ecosystem which embraces its rock, soil, climate, topography, and the influences of its marine location, is precious.

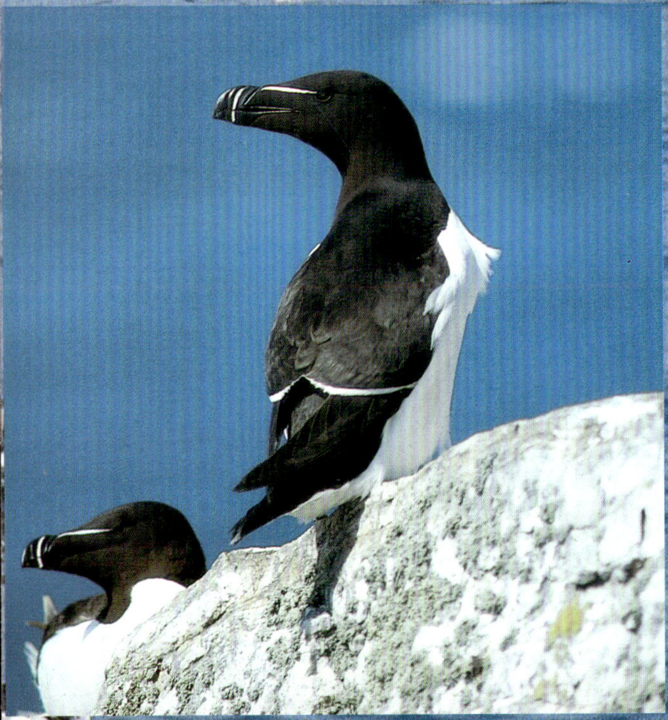

Razorbill

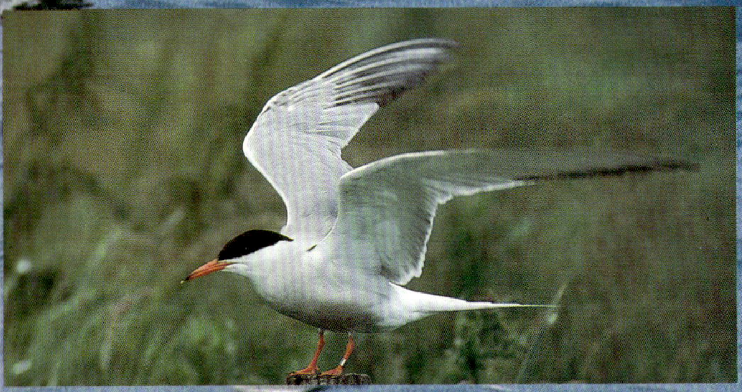

Common Tern

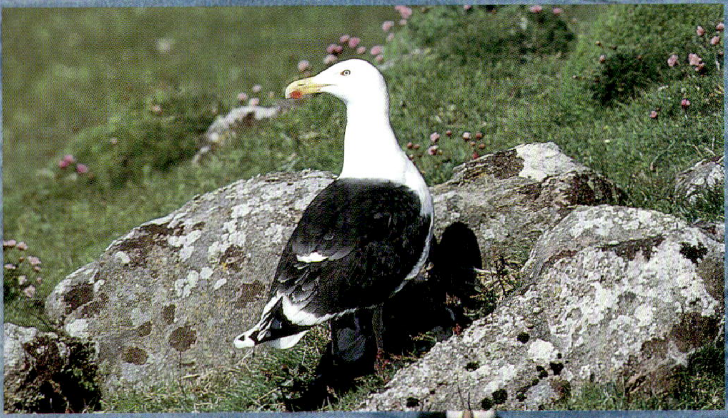

Great Black Backed Gull

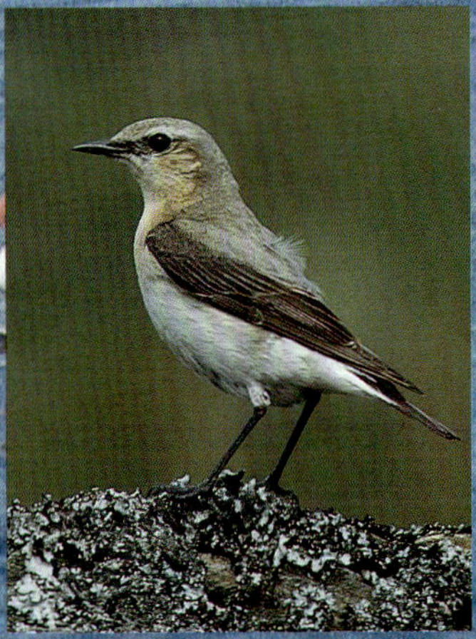

Wheatear

ACCESS TO THE ISLAND

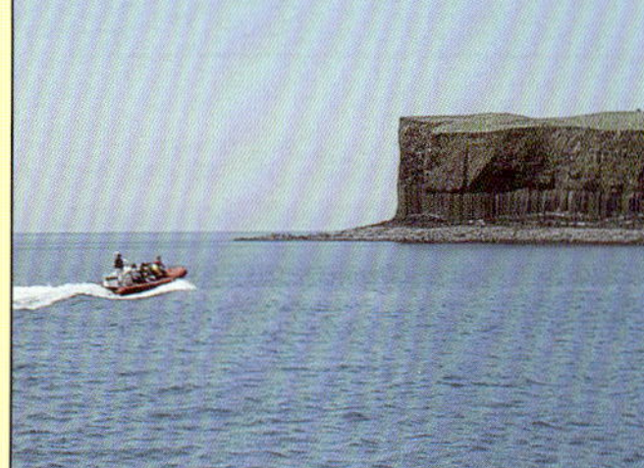

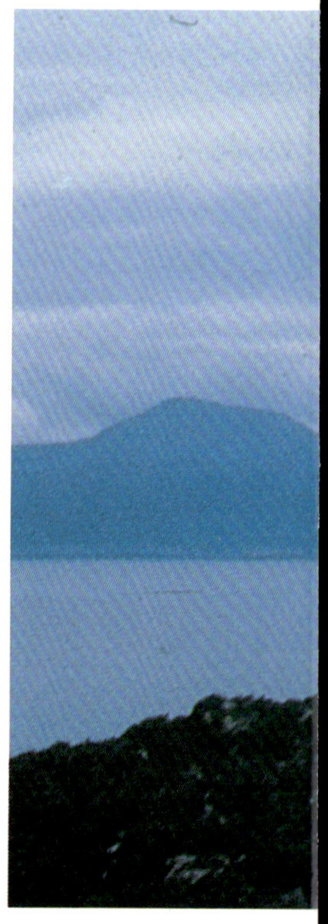

Early visitors to Staffa had to make their own arangements for reaching the island, or prevail upon their hosts to do so for them. Many crossed from Ulva, six miles north-east of Staffa, engaging boatmen in what was then a well-populated area.

In the 1820's a paddle steamer based in Glasgow started making weekly voyages in summer to Iona and Staffa; and from the 1840's steamboats from Oban would sail round Mull calling at the two islands, taking 15 or 16 hours for the circuit.

The means of transporting people to Staffa improved in regularity, speed and comfort over the years, although the services were provided continuously until 1931 by paddle steamers, with passengers being put ashore in ships' boats.

The 800-passenger MacBrayne turbine steamer 'King George V' took over the daily round-Mull sailings in 1935, billing them "The Sacred Isles cruise". Apart from the war years she landed people on Staffa, on calm days, by ferrying them in launches.

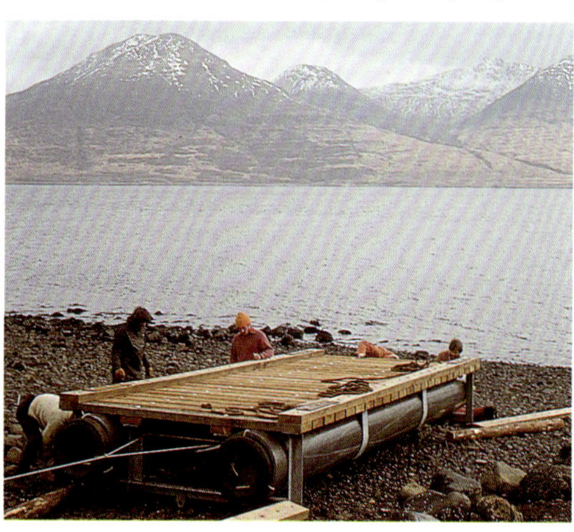

Assembling one of the pontoons for the floating jetty.

These landings were stopped in 1967 because of the time they took, and because of anxiety about rock falls on the Causeway. Then, in 1974, the 50-year old 'King George V' was withdrawn, leaving Staffa more isolated than it had been for over 100 years.

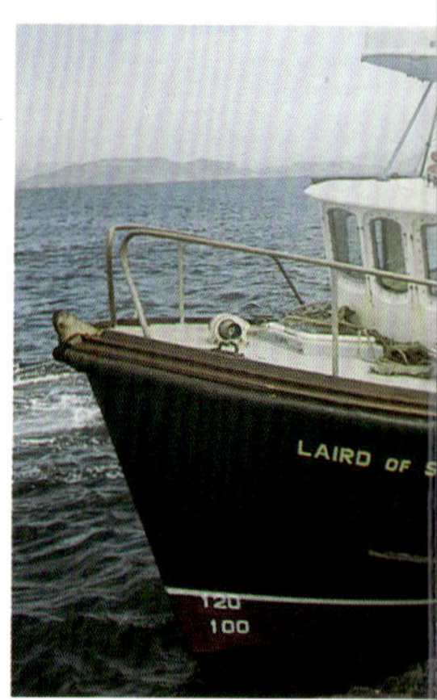

Passengers embarking on the launch 'Laird of Staffa' for a visit to the island.

Thereafter several operators of small craft on Mull and Iona set out to satisfy the ever-present desire of visitors from all over the world to get to Staffa. They offered the prospect, in most cases, of landing whenever the weather was settled; though securing a boat alongside slippery rock in even a gentle swell calls for skill and patience on the part of the crew as well as trust in the surefootedness of the passengers. In 1976 an attempt was made to provide a floating jetty for use by these craft: it was to be chained to the island each summer, and towed to a sheltered anchorage on Mull for the winter. However, trials showed it to behave erratically in some sea states, and it was not brought into use.

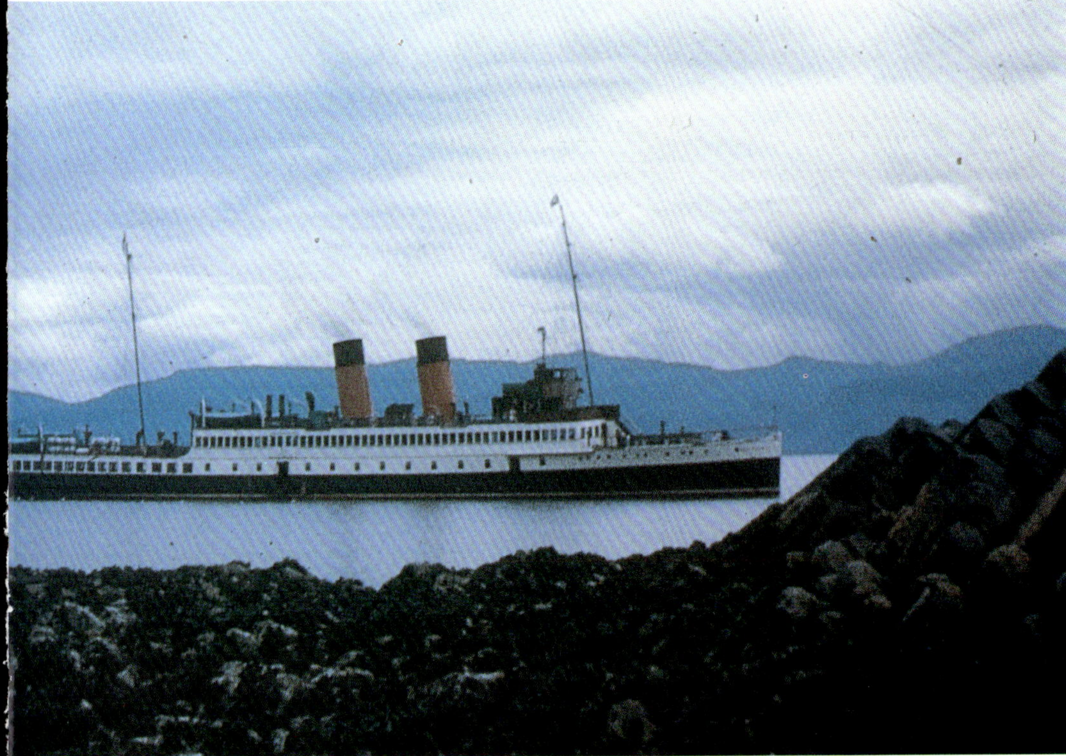

T.S. 'King George V' lying off the mouth of Fingal's Cave.

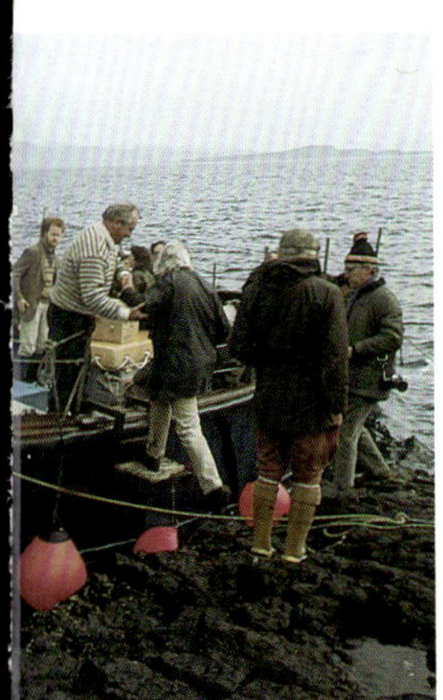

Real advance in the facilities for landing on Staffa only came when The National Trust for Scotland invested in the design and construction of a steel and concrete landing stage at Clamshell Cave, completed in 1991. Now, at last, there is a properly-engineered site at which small vessels can discharge passengers on to the island.

Once ashore most visitors want to explore the plateau. Although scrambling up the cliff beside Clamshell Cave has always been possible, owners have tended to discourage the practice as being too risky. For much of the time that people have been coming to Staffa there has been some kind of stairway. When the King of Saxony came in 1844 he reported using new wooden stairs there. By 1885 they had become delapidated and were replaced; but the new flight was removed in 1937 by MacBraynes who wanted to try and restrict their passengers to the Causeway and Fingal's Cave. Then, in 1977, a concrete and aluminium stairway, intended to be a permanent and safe way up and down, was installed.

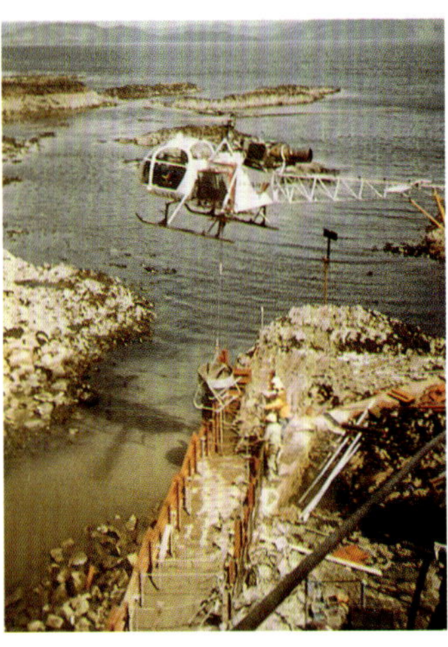

A helicopter helping in the construction of the new jetty in 1990.

Several places issue their own stamps. They do this either to pay for the cost of carrying mail in areas where there is no official postal service; or simply to provide a form of souvenir. Such stamps are properly called *carriage labels* or *Cinderella issues*. Here in UK they are of no interest to the Inland Revenue, and they are ignored by the Post Office.

STAFFA STAMPS

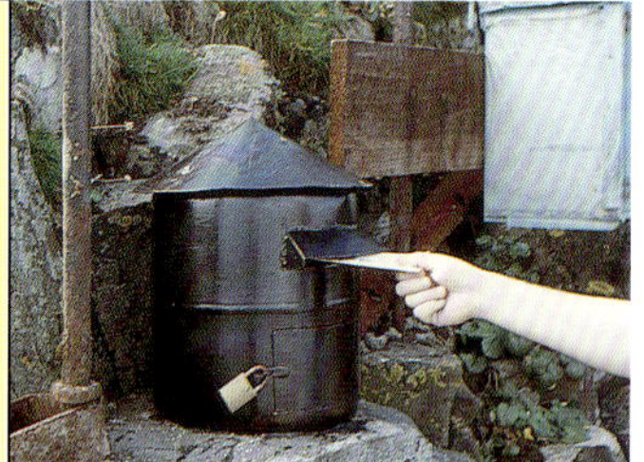

Staffa stamps, introduced in 1968, were sold by the boatman who used to take visitors from Iona and Fionnphort out to Staffa in his motor boat. Then in 1974 the owner of the island appointed a contractor to design, produce and supply new sets of stamps. Some examples of his work are illustrated here.

In 1976, when the launch 'Laird of Staffa' came into service, a robust weatherproof letter-box was installed at Clamshell Cave. Passengers could then buy postcards and Staffa stamps on board on the trip out to Staffa, post their mail in the letter-box, and have it collected, franked on the return voyage, and handed in at a post office on Mull.

This arrangement worked well at first. It ended after two years when the contractor, in an excess of zeal, decided to issue Staffa stamps in each of the twelve New England states to commemorate the bi-centenary of America's independence. Now, after a decent interval, the stamps could be reintroduced locally.

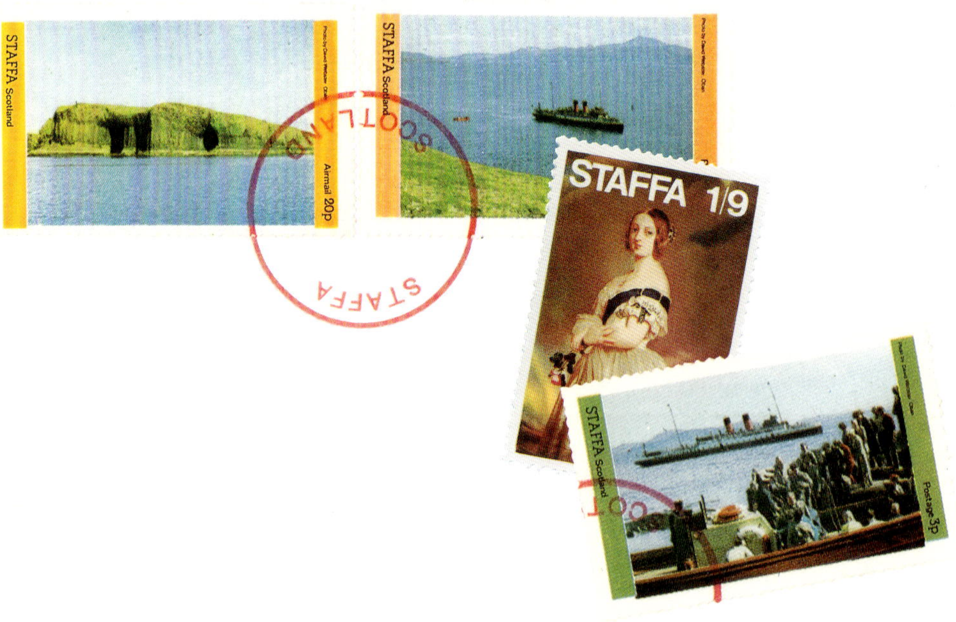